CONTAINER GARDENING

CONTAINER GARDENING

Series Concept: Robert J. Dolezal
Encyclopedia Concept: Barbara K. Dolezal
Managing Editor: Louise Damberg
Copy Editors: Nancy Strege, Kathy Talley-Jones
Photography Editor: John M. Rickard
Designer: Jerry Simon
Layout Artists: Rik Boyd, Andrea Reider
Photoshop Artist: Ryan Pressler
Horticulturists: Carrie Heinley, Peggy Henry, Kathy Talley-Jones
Photo Stylists: Joyce M. Almstad, Carrie Heinley, Peggy Henry
Research: Shelley Ring Diamond
Index: Rick Hurd

President/CEO: David D. Murphy
Vice President/Editorial: Patricia K. Jacobsen
Vice President/Retail Sales & Marketing: Richard M. Miller

Home Improvement/*Gardening*
Executive Editor: Bryan Trandem
Editorial Director: Jerri Farris
Creative Director: Tim Himsel

Created by: Dolezal & Associates,
in partnership with Creative Publishing international, Inc.,
in cooperation with Black & Decker.
BLACK&DECKER is a trademark of the Black & Decker
Corporation and is used under license.

Library of Congress
Cataloging-in-Publication Data

(Information on file)

ISBN 0–86573–438–0 (hardcover)
ISBN 0–86573–442–9 (softcover)

PHOTOGRAPHY & ILLUSTRATION

PRINCIPAL PHOTOGRAPHY

JOHN RICKARD: Cover and pgs. *iv* (top, 2nd from top & bot), *vi*, 3 (top L & top R), 4 (top L), 5 (top), 6, 7 (top), 9 (top), 10, 15 (top & mid), 16, 20 (top), 28 (top L & bot), 29 (top), 30 (bot L & bot R), 31, 32 (bot), 33, 34, 36, 37, 38 (bot), 39, 40, 48 (top), 50 (top), 52 (top), 58, 62, 64, 65, 66 (top), 67, 68, 70 (top L), 71, 72, 73 (top R), 74 (bot), 75 (bot & steps 1–3), 76 (bot R), 77, 80 (bot R & bot L), 81, 82, 86, 87, 88 (top L), 90 (bot L & bot R), 92, 94 (bot L & bot R), 95 (bot), 96, 100 (bot), 102 (top), 104 (mid), 105 (bot), 106 (bot), 107 (bot), 108 (mid & bot), 113 (top & bot), 114, 116 (bot), 118 (bot), 119 (bot), 121 (bot), 122 (top & bot), 123 (top), 126 (top), 127 (mid), 129 (top)

OTHER PHOTOGRAPHY AND ILLUSTRATION

TIM BUTLER: pgs. 2 (bot), 4 (top R & bot), 5 (mid), 11, 14 (top), 15 (bot), 17, 18, 22 (bot L & bot R), 32 (top), 35, 73 (top L, mid L, & bot L), 76 (mid L), 78 (top L & mid L), 79 (bot), 80 (top), 84, 85, 90 (top), 93 (top), 98 (mid), 99 (top & bot), 100 (top), 101 (top & bot), 102 (mid), 105 (top & mid), 106 (mid), 107 (mid), 108 (top), 109 (top & bot), 110, 111 (mid), 112 (top), 113 (mid), 117, 120 (top), 121 (top), 123 (mid), 124 (mid & bot), 125 (top & bot), 127 (bot), 128 (mid & bot), 129 (mid)

KYLE CHESSER: pgs. *iv* (3rd from top), *v* (top, 2nd & 3rd from top), *vii*, 19 (bot), 20 (bot), 21, 22 (top L & top R), 42, 43 (bot: step 3), 44, 45, 48 (bot), 49, 52 (bot), 53, 54 (bot), 55, 59, 63, 70 (bot), 73 (bot R), 75 (top & steps 1–2), 95 (top)

CREATIVE PUBLISHING INTERNATIONAL: pgs. 8 (bot L), 12, 19 (top), 46, 54 (top), 74 (top), 76 (top L), 98 (top), 102 (bot), 103 (mid), 112 (mid & bot)

CORBIS/KEN WILSON: pg. 129 (bot)

DOUG DEALEY: pgs. 2 (top), 5 (bot), 8 (mid L & bot R), 14 (mid), 88 (top R & bot L), 94 (top), 115 (mid)

REED ESTABROOK: pgs. 7 (bot), 26, 30 (top), 61 (bot)

DAVID GOLDBERG: pgs. 7 (mid), 14 (bot)

SAXON HOLT: pgs. 50 (bot), 51, 98 (bot), 99 (mid), 103 (top), 107 (top), 111 (bot), 116 (mid), 118 (top & mid), 119 (top & mid), 120 (mid & bot), 122 (mid), 124 (top), 126 (bot), 128 (top)

IMAGEPOINT: pgs. *v* (bot), 9 (bot), 23, 28 (top R), 29 (bot), 38 (top), 43 (top & steps 1–3), 47, 56, 57, 61 (top), 66 (bot), 70 (top R), 78 (top R, mid R & bot R), 79 (top), 88 (bot R), 89, 91, 93 (bot), 100 (mid), 104 (bot), 106 (top), 115 (top)

CHARLES NUCCI: pg. 115 (bot)

PAM PEIRCE: pg. 76 (bot L)

PHOTODISC IMAGE STOCK: pg. 3 (bot)

CHARLES SLAY: pgs. 104 (top), 111 (top), 116 (top), 123 (bot), 126 (mid), 127 (top)

YVONNE WILLIAMS: pgs. 60, 101 (mid), 103 (bot)

ILLUSTRATIONS: HILDEBRAND DESIGN

The editors acknowledge with grateful appreciation the contribution to this book of Alden Lane Nursery, Livermore, California, and the cooperation of Betsy Niles and Anita Tommasi, Sonoma, California.

CONTAINER GARDENING

Author
Rich Binsacca

Photographer
John M. Rickard

Series Concept
Robert J. Dolezal

CREATIVE
PUBLISHING
international

Minnetonka, Minnesota

C O N T E N T S

PLANTING IN CONTAINERS

Page 41

CARING FOR CONTAINER GARDENS

Page 69

DECORATING WITH CONTAINERS

Page 83

ENCYCLOPEDIA OF CONTAINER PLANTS

Page 97

APPENDIX

Page 131

FOREWORD

y mother is the classic container gardener. While the hill behind my parents' house supports an orchard and an annual vegetable garden (and once a thriving ollaliberry patch), it is the narrow slab of concrete patio along the back of the house that is her true love.

There she maintains about 30 potted plants—a lemon tree, a big rhododendron, roses, and a host of annual flowers and perennial shrubs—in wine barrels, long wood planters and clay pots, among other vessels and containers.

*There is a garden
in every childhood,
an enchanted place
where colors are brighter,
the air softer, and
the morning more
fragrant than ever again.*

Elizabeth Lawrence

When I set out to write this book, what struck me was that my mom had never read a book about container gardening (until now) or even discussed the subject at length with a gardener at the local nursery or home center. Not that she couldn't benefit from such sources, but she has become comfortable gardening by trial and error, tending her plantings with care and diligence. The depth and breadth of her container garden is a testament to her passion for it. Yes, she makes mistakes—and understands that doing so is part of the container gardening experience, part of both the fun and the challenge.

For her—and others, I think—container gardening is a little like raising children. Consider how contained plants are almost always kept nearby, within view, to be both nurtured and enjoyed. Potted plants require constant care, with the work tiring but rewarding, and rarely tedious. There's always something to do. You watch as seeds burst from the ground, foliate, and flower, or as a tree or shrub grows and spreads, eventually requiring a new container or a permanent place to thrive.

It is parenting at its best.

I t's little wonder that so many gardeners increasingly are drawn to planting in containers. The reasons and benefits are as many and varied as the types of containers and plants available.

One obvious reason for container gardening's popularity is space, or the lack of it—but it's harder to explain why even folks with open gardens choose to keep plants in containers. The fact is, potted plants add vigor and value to any space.

For practicality, containers are a good choice. Container gardens give you greater control over soil conditions. With the proper container, potted plants can be mobile, allowing the garden to be protected easily from inclement weather—and letting the gardener maintain plantings in garden locations that otherwise would not sustain them.

In addition, when you go on vacation, having your garden conveniently grouped—and mobile—makes it oh-so-much-easier for a kindly neighbor to care for it. Mostly, a container garden allows you to grow plantings that are foreign to your soil and climate and to express your personal style. If your tastes or needs change, so can your plantings, quickly and easily.

Successful container gardening actually requires a bit more knowledge and care than a typical in-ground garden, especially if you are experimenting with unusual plants or you live in an extreme climate. It's vital to match the right plantings to the right container. This marriage can be successful with the proper preparation, the right soil mix, and some extra care and feeding.

> **Opening up entire new worlds of possibilities can be counted among container gardening's enduring virtues**

The Simple Pleasures of Container Gardening

The wide variety of plants and containers available makes selection an exciting process limited only by your imagination.

SMALL-SPACE GARDENS

Of all the reasons to keep plants in pots, perhaps the best is the ability of container gardens to enhance spaces that are limited and bring intimacy to spaces that are vast. Small-space gardens appeal to not only gardeners with just a small patch of patio, a narrow balcony, or a front stoop; they're also ideal for gardeners seeking to add focus to a large landscape.

Consider the possibilities: a windowbox with just a passing glance at sunlight can welcome violas and lobelia. Blank patio walls suddenly become complete when hanging baskets are added, filled with geraniums and petunias. The garden bench under the shade tree becomes even more inviting when nestled up to a 27-gallon (100-l) half whiskey barrel filled with cherry tomatoes ripe for the picking. A long planter box filled with salvia, sweet alyssum, and asters guides guests down the garden path to a backyard barbecue or poolside gathering.

Container gardens also are as practical as they are beautiful. Dwarf fruit trees or a trellis sporting a full bloom of sweet peas can shield areas needing privacy—or hide views that are unsightly. A strategic arrangement of pots containing wisteria or roses will soften the starkness of a water meter, a heating oil fill pipe, or an air-conditioning unit.

In many ways, the small-space garden represents the secret wish of most gardeners—to fill every nook and cranny of available horizontal and vertical space, and to make of this world…a garden.

An array of hanging planters and baskets complements the garden bed below, drawing the eye above ground level and adding color and life to an otherwise neutral and empty surface.

Container gardening allows you to experiment with non-native plants and interesting container shapes and materials.

For most gardeners, the love of planting extends beyond the back door to the indoor world, where seeds are cultivated, young plants are protected from the elements, and the bounty of an onion or potato harvest is stored.

INDOOR GARDENING

Indoor container gardening is a natural extension of this passion, allowing the gardener to enjoy the scents and textures of a living garden inside the home, year-round. From sunrooms filled with tropical trees to kitchen cabinets draped in the vines of a philodendron, a home is an accommodating environment for many potted plants.

Gardening indoors offers as many possibilities as in-ground planting—just on a smaller scale and with a few different considerations. Although the space in a container is limited, you'll be surprised at how many spots you can adorn with potted plants. Container plants also provide a health benefit, producing oxygen while absorbing carbon dioxide, poisonous

(Left and above) Indoors or out, container gardening allows close-knit combinations of various plant textures and shapes to match equally unusual pots.

carbon monoxide, and other airborne toxins through photosynthesis.

The major need of indoor plants is attention to watering. Forced-air systems can dry out an indoor plant, especially if it is located near a vent, because the hot air these systems produce is low in humidity; make sure you check on the dryness of the soil daily and water accordingly. Most containers are set on saucers, but if water is allowed to stand in a saucer, the roots of the plant will rot. An easy solution for plants that require regular, light watering is to fill a leak-proof bucket or other vessel with water and "wick" it to the plant through capillary tubes.

Indoor plants, such as this African violet, can subtly complement dramatic architectural elements.

MINIATURE GARDENS

The beauty and distinctive growth and blooming patterns of miniature and dwarf-variety plants and flowers often can get lost in a large, open garden, but they are perfectly suited to container gardening.

The very nature of container gardening makes smaller blooms and finer foliage more visible. Many flowering miniature varieties bloom in tight clusters, creating unusual bouquets of cutting flowers and adding interest and variety to an arrangement of larger plantings. A miniature garden tableau, employing dwarf shrubs, bonsai, and mosses or other ground covers, along with tiny flowering perennials and annuals, can replicate a much larger scheme in the coziness and intimacy of a container.

(Above) Hardy bonsai trees are a popular miniature, requiring little water and room for roots. Their essence is the ability to capture a landscape in diminutive form.

On a more practical note, the smaller root systems and reduced nutritional needs of miniatures and dwarf varieties make them better suited than their full-size brethren to the confines of a container. They're also easier to prune, given their diminutive stature at full maturity.

In fact, the growing popularity of container gardening has accelerated the development of miniature and dwarf plants, with a wide range of choices in almost every category and species.

(Top) With a large enough pot, you can create a mini-garden that's also mobile.

(Left) Water gardens, anchored by water lilies and native grasses, attract attention—and an amazing variety of animal life—to the garden.

HANGING PLANTS

When many people think of a container garden, the first thing that comes to mind is a pot or other grounded vessel. Thinking vertical—in the form of hanging baskets—offers a host of opportunities to add color, attract attention, and express your personal style.

Suspended from sidewalls; beside door openings; along verandas, garden paths, or deep arbors; and even from tree branches, hanging baskets bring color and texture to eye level as well as to points above and below. They allow you to continue the theme of other garden plantings or contrast with them.

On the practical side, plants at waist or eye level often are easier to water and care for than are those planted in the ground. You may be able to spot pests earlier when they're staring right back at you or see the signs of illness at an earlier stage. For gardeners with physical limitations—or folks who just prefer not to crouch or dirty their knees—plants potted along a deck railing, under a window, or alongside a door frame allow full enjoyment of gardening with greater ease and less effort.

A major consideration of hanging plants, of course, is their weight. While this can be somewhat controlled by using wire baskets, moss, and lightweight soil mix, a fully planted and watered container can be hefty. Make sure you use durable chains, hooks, and wires, as well as heavy-duty fasteners. Secure baskets to structural components, such as the beams of a covered porch, deck posts, or the studs of a sidewall or door frame.

Before you plant the basket and buy the hardware, suspend the container where you want it, then check to make sure the container itself is not out of scale for the space. Keep in mind that if you intend to plant trailers and climbers, especially, they will add dimension to the finished basket.

(Top left) Open baskets usually are lined with sphagnum moss to contain soil and help retain moisture, while reducing weight.

(Above) Hanging plants are even appropriate for an open garden, in this case filling the space beneath a low-lying tree limb.

Hanging baskets placed along vertical surfaces can break up the monotony of a facade or draw the eye to an architectural feature of the home.

EDIBLE TREASURES

One of the great advantages of container gardening is the proximity of the gardener to the plants, which usually are just outside a door or window and sometimes are right inside the house. Proximity is especially sweet (or tangy, or juicy, or aromatic) when a plant yields an edible treasure.

Herbs, leafy greens, root vegetables, and tomatoes are common container vegetables, while strawberries lead the fruit pack. Most often, the popularity of these plants for containers has to do with their growth rates and yield. Chives and lemon balm, for instance, can provide a quick yield in a very small space, such as a windowbox, a "parsley pot" (a multitiered vertical container), or a long, thin planter along a balcony railing. Tomatoes can grow from a compact pot to climb a lattice or trellis, thus conserving space yet producing the same yield as plants that take up more space in an open garden.

The produce from fruit-bearing plants enhances both the dinner table and the gardener's experience. It's simply a gardener's unmatched delight to be able to reach out a window for a sprig of basil or mint, unlatch the back door to harvest a handful of lettuce leaves, or look on the balcony and see a ripening array of yellow, green, and red peppers. Is it any wonder that fruits and vegetables have a long history of surviving and thriving in containers?

(Below) Popular for their color and tempting yield, strawberries are an easy edible to grow in containers, such as a Mexican strawberry pot.

(Below) Cherry or miniature tomatoes can thrive in larger pots, putting them near at hand to the kitchen and the cook; as with any vegetable grown in containers, the best bet for success are found among dwarf varieties.

(Above) Herbs offer an aroma and texture that complement any garden (and any meal). They're an ideal companion for locations outside the kitchen door.

If you want to bring a tree into closer proximity, a landscape container is probably part of the plan. Like the plants they hold, these structural containers can serve many purposes, from providing plenty of space for large-root plants (or several plants in the same planting) to serving double duty as extra seating,

LANDSCAPE CONTAINERS

flanking an entry, or helping to define areas of a larger garden or yard.

Landscape containers have all the advantages of other containers but offer more gardening space. They can be built into the structure of a raised wood deck or concrete patio, providing dimension and focus to an otherwise flat, geometric surface. Small or dwarf-variety trees are an obvious choice for these large pots, and their volume will support just about any planting your hardiness zone can handle, including blending bedding plants, nurturing a perennial or shrub for an eventual move to the open garden, growing vegetables, or cultivating miniature roses.

Landscape containers are available in a variety of materials and styles from nurseries

and home garden centers; also check out salvage yards for large tubs and cisterns that can be converted into interesting or whimsical containers.

If there is one thing that ardent container gardeners believe, it is this: anything that can hold soil is a potential pot. Of course, there are considerations regarding the viability of any potential planter [see Selecting Containers, pg. 17], but your choices are limited only by your imagination.

(Top left) Building an elevated brick planter not only adds permanence to your garden but puts colorful annuals in better view.

(Above) A slope terraced with retaining walls offers a good opportunity for displaying container plants.

The tops of rock or stone walls— here with some capstones carved out to accommodate ground covers and other low-lying plants—provide the perfect stage for potted plants.

WHIMSICAL GARDENS

For sheer whimsy's sake, there's value in going off the beaten path and bringing home an old boot, battle-worn helmet, chimney pot, or sink basin from an antique store, preparing it properly, filling it with potting soil, and planting it with—whatever you love most.

If budget is a consideration, take another look at that rusty old wagon, long since relegated to the basement or attic clutter, and picture it as a home to flowers or an herb bed. The spokes of that old bicycle could be fashioned as a lattice for climbing vines. The rungs of a rickety stepladder may be still secure enough to bear a few lightweight pots of flowers. Unusual containers are at the heart of the personal sense of style and statement that container gardeners bring to their potted gardens.

Besides form and function, such containers also offer an environmental benefit—that of reusing and recycling materials and products that otherwise would end up in landfills or as discards polluting the landscape.

However, the dash of surprise that whimsical containers can add to a garden should be limited to just that: a dash. A patio covered with old boots sprouting petunias can quickly go from being a conversation topic to a source of whispered concern about one's sanity. A few well-selected, nontraditional planters will have the best impact in high-visibility areas.

Novelty aside, all containers need to fit the bill as proper planters, including the ability to hold soil, drain water, take in oxygen, survive the elements, and generally promote the growth and health of the plants they hold.

(Below) A bicycle built for two—potted plants, that is—epitomizes the limitless possibilities of appropriate, well-prepared containers.

(Bottom left) Old picnic baskets are great for annual flowers, allowing you to move the flowers around the garden, to the front porch, or even inside.

(Right) Imagination is the key to creating a memorable and eye-catching container garden.

CONTAINER GARDEN GIFTS

When creating a container garden gift, all you need as your guide are a little creativity, a sense of style, and the occasion itself. If you primarily are an outdoor gardener, creating a container gift also allows you to try something new and work on a different scale. Here are just a few ideas:

- **Hanging baskets.** Dramatic and impressive, a hanging basket flowing with annual and perennial climbers, trailers, and bushy foliage makes an eye-catching and long-lasting housewarming gift. To save the recipient from a trip to the hardware store, include the requisite hooks, chains, and fasteners.

- **Holiday tree.** A potted miniature or immature evergreen, decorated for the season, can brighten a dining room table or buffet, a fireplace mantel, or even the front stoop, then be transplanted to a larger pot or to open ground after the last frost.

- **Personalized container.** Decorate or glaze a terra-cotta pot with personal messages or informative and entertaining gardening tips. Transform a unique or nontraditional container that fits a friend's personality, garden, or home decor, and fill it with a perennial for lasting value.

- **Starter set.** Package together the essentials: a container, seeds or starters from your own garden, soil mix, nutrients, and maybe a trowel. Such sets are great for children and novice gardeners looking to gain experience and confidence; if you give annuals (for faster and more dramatic results), be sure to mention their single-season cycle.

- **Terrarium.** A forgotten indoor treasure, terrariums are appropriate for almost any environment, providing a bit of nature in a small package. Use an unusual fish bowl or other clear glassware to house the plants.

- **Small box of herbs.** For cooks and indoor gardeners with a greenhouse window, a shallow box or clay dish of three to four different herbs is an aromatic and functional gift.

- **Fruit or vegetable harvest.** Container gardens may not yield as much as trees or vegetable plants in an open garden, but a small basket of homegrown produce—a head of lettuce, a few tomatoes, perhaps a dwarf lemon—makes an impressive and tasty gift.

With any live garden gift, include care instructions, especially if the recipient is a novice gardener or a child. Offer your services, too—sharing your enthusiasm for gardening is the best part of this gift and will deepen any relationship.

(Left) A bouquet of annuals in a sturdy container allows you to pass along the bounty of your garden to others.

(Below) Simple arrangements, like this urn of cloverlike shamrocks, are easy to create and have lasting beauty.

GARDENS TO ATTRACT BIRDS AND BUTTERFLIES

What's a garden of flowers without butterflies flitting about, or a tree without a nest of birds? As you plan your container garden and select the plants you'll grow, consider choosing some varieties that attract our winged friends to their nectar and foliage.

Container gardens bring these "flying flowers" up close, allowing you to view them from a window sill or garden bench, enjoy their playful antics, and watch them feed and drink from your bounty. If you've planted shrubs or trees, your blessings may extend to an intimate observation of birds' nesting habits and progeny.

Butterflies are attracted to bright colors and nectar-rich flowers such as pink petta, red salvia, and lantana—a hardy, easy-to-manage variety with small, colorful flowers (often in combination) that bloom in tight clusters against a deep green backdrop of broad, textured foliage. Birds enjoy this perennial as well, and in moderate, frost-free climates, it blooms nearly year-round.

In addition to flowers and their nectar, you can provide other food sources. Butterfly larvae, or caterpillars, need something to munch on (such as potted parsley) before they cocoon; larvae also provide food for birds, as do beneficial bugs brought in to grub on destructive garden pests.

Installing other garden attractions, including feeders, birdhouses, water gardens, and birdbaths, will welcome visitors to your plants while adding yet another enjoyable facet to your container garden.

(Right) Annual and perennial flowers often provide camouflage for butterflies, sometimes as colorful as the flowers themselves.

(Left) Nectar from a flowering tree or perennial offers birds a steady source of nutrition. As regular visitors to your garden, birds provide natural pest control against boring bugs and other threats or, as in the case of this hummingbird, simple yet fascinating beauty.

(Opposite) Besides providing shelter for your feathered friends, birdhouses can add an attractive feature to your garden in the bower beneath a potted tree.

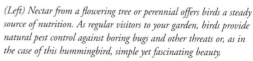

Even though there is much information on container gardening available—in print, online, and over the broadcast airwaves—the truth is, most gardeners in the potted realm do it by the seat of their pants. Trial and error is the most common learning method, sometimes stimulated by a quick glance at a neighbor's porch pots, spotting a new cultivar at the garden center, or casual discussions with fellow gardeners.

Taking this tack surely has its upside (experimentation is half the fun, after all); unfortunately, there also is a downside, usually experienced as a lack of consistent success. Though in many respects container gardens are easier to prepare and tend than open gardens, there are other ways in which they can be more demanding, particularly if your choice of plantings and containers is not carefully considered.

Plan, prepare, and choose form and function— they're key to every successful container garden

A Garden Checklist

That's the driving force behind this chapter and the Container Gardening Planning Flowchart [see pg. 24]. Together, these tools can help direct your choices of containers and plantings, soil and nutrients, and climate and conditions, so that success is assured.

Spending some time with this checklist also will help you refine and define the reasons you want to plant in pots, then guide you as you choose a site, select containers, and plant and care for your flowers, shrubs, and trees. Finally, you'll get tips about the tools, materials, and resources needed to start and maintain your container garden.

Container gardening involves more than just a plant and a pot; it also requires the right soil mix and the proper tools to achieve success.

CHOOSING A SITE

The benefit of a container garden is that every location is truly appropriate, from urban rooftops and balconies (right and bottom) to the deck railing of a suburban home (below).

In many cases, the location for your container garden already will have suggested itself. In other cases, your desire for certain plantings may be your primary motivation; in other words, you have a pot in search of a spot.

In either case, you'll want to know more before making a trip to the local nursery or garden center. The first consideration is whether the container garden will be placed indoors or out. Next, consider the basic physical parameters of the space, such as the dimensions of the patio, deck, entry, roof terrace, or other setting, including that area's structural capabilities. If you choose an outside location, consider the climate and the area's exposure to wind and rain, sun and shade. Follow the sun throughout the day to figure out when the plantings will receive full sun exposure and when shade, keeping in mind that this will change with the progression of the seasons (calculate this for indoor containers, too).

Next, decide whether the container should be moveable to protect it from the elements or to provide it with better sun exposure at different times of the year. You also may want to choose an area that's close to a regular source of water. Container plantings dry out faster than their in-ground counterparts—in fact, underwatering is the primary malady that afflicts potted plants. Considering all of these issues will help you choose the proper plantings and suggest places where they will thrive.

As long as there's the right amount of sun and protection from other elements (such as wind, especially on a rooftop), almost any site can provide a stage for a container garden.

Deciding why you want to garden in containers is a key consideration, affecting your choice of plants, not to mention your choice of the containers themselves. The potential reasons are many and varied, so start by writing down your every reason for wanting to create a container garden.

GARDENS FOR EVERY PURPOSE

For example, do you simply enjoy the pleasure of working with soil? If so, is a container garden an addition to your outdoor gardening efforts or a substitute for them? Are you interested in container gardening to generate starter shoots and protect young saplings until they're strong enough to weather both storms and sunshine in an open garden, or is it basically your only gardening option? Are you looking to try out some new or non-native plantings in a more controlled environment, or are you seeking to enhance your outdoor landscape with decorative objects?

Potted annuals make a stunning complement to an open garden, adding bright colors to a backdrop of evergreen foliage or leading folks exploring down a garden path.

Perhaps the vast array of containers and the ability to mix and match them to create a unique look appeals to you, especially as an option for gift giving. You may want to extend your growing season by moving containers inside or to other yard locations where your favorite plantings will thrive longer. Maybe it's as simple as the fact that you'll soon be moving and you want to take certain plantings with you to your new home.

Whatever your reasons, be aware that contained gardens can require more maintenance than open gardens, especially if they're located indoors. If you've listed "because I don't have time for an open garden" among your reasons, always select the hardiest and least-demanding plants and pots you can find—they'll be essential to your success.

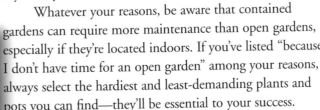

Whether as a tabletop display (inset) or a screen to create privacy for a seating area, potted plants offer a variety of forms and functional benefits.

SCALING THE PROJECT

The scale and complexity of your container garden depends on several factors, including the amount of time you have to devote to it, your skills as a gardener, your budget, and your chosen garden location.

If you're unsure of your skills and schedule, it's a good idea to start small, with hardy, native plants that require minimal maintenance or special care. For instance, a potted tree may seem daunting because of its size, but the right species can be a simple way to add an impressive element to your garden. A single windowbox of annuals, perhaps mixed in with enduring perennials, requires upfront work and periodic care throughout the blooming season, but it isn't a year-round project. By contrast, managing a potted fruit tree or nursing a non-native plant is a more ambitious venture, requiring a higher degree of skill and sufficient time to be successful.

The scale of your garden also requires consideration of available space. You may want to fill your balcony with annual color in small or varying-sized pots, for instance, but doing so might eliminate a favorite summer reading spot or create a storage problem for all those containers (as well as your tools and materials) when the growing season ends.

An arrangement of annuals might be just the ticket, delivering dramatic color for a single season with limited effort on your part.

Similarly, a patio or deck flowing with low-level foliage may be manageable from a time standpoint but will reduce the area's usable space for outdoor gatherings and also may be subject to damage from playful children and pets. As an alternative, hang containers from railings, posts, walls, or other vertical surfaces.

When calculating your time, think about how much you have to commit to container gardening, then reduce it by half. If you're soon left twiddling your thumbs after your first trip to the nursery or garden center, you can always scale up your efforts. As you gain confidence from success on a smaller scale, you'll probably want to spend more time in the garden, but if you start out too aggressively and watch your plants wither from neglect or inexperience, it's easy to become discouraged.

For novice container gardeners, the key is to start small, gain confidence, then expand your garden as your skill and imagination permit.

Tour any nursery or garden center—even a salvage yard or garage sale—and you'll get a sense of just how many containers and potential containers are out there. By the most liberal definition, a plant container is anything that will hold enough soil and provide adequate drainage to support the health and growth of a given plant. Under that directive, everything from a clay pot to a truck tire (drilled with drain holes, of course) is fair game.

With regard to containers, perhaps the most important question is, which comes first—the plant or the pot? If you have specific plants in mind for your garden, their size, growth potential, and soil and water needs often dictate the types of containers that best will support them. Conversely, if you fall in love with a suitable container first, its construction and capabilities will suggest the types of plants that will do well in it.

For some locations, such as raised wood decks and roof terraces, you may have to consider the overall weight of the contained plant. A pot's shape also may suggest its use: tapered containers are easier to lift and carry; large and square vessels offer better support for plants with extensive root systems because they hold more soil and thus maintain a higher volume of water and nutrient reserves.

Within these boundaries is a wide range of style options; it mostly comes down to a matter of personal taste. While it certainly is prudent to reject a container that is poorly suited to planting, don't rule it out just because it's not immediately attractive. The shape, size, material, texture, imperfections, degree of wear, placement, and even the plants you choose can transform what otherwise might be considered eccentric into an intriguing and beautiful container.

SELECTING CONTAINERS

Metal containers, unless designed specifically to hold plants, usually must be drilled to provide proper drainage holes, treated, and cleaned to avoid soil, disease, and root problems.

That said, quality and durability are the key concerns. An old wood-framed foot locker can become an interesting planter, but its useful life depends on how well you can protect it from rot by properly lining the inside and raising it off the ground. Similarly, an inexpensive, thin plastic pot, purchased in a moment of frugality, may not survive the winter or stand up to a gust of wind. As a general rule, buy the best you can afford for the plants you select; that policy is applicable to all gardening components, including soil, containers, tools, and the plants themselves.

COMMON CONTAINER MATERIALS

Most garden containers are made from natural materials such as wood, terra cotta, and stone, which complement the natural quality of a garden. There is an almost unlimited range of styles, sizes, shapes, and cost choices among these materials.

- **Wood.** A natural insulator, wood protects roots from cold. Even though it's porous, wood retains moisture better than unglazed terra cotta. It balances moisture and air without allowing the soil to dry out too quickly.

  Wood, however, is susceptible to rot. To slow that process, containers should drain properly. Direct water away from the planter and raise it about an inch (25 mm) aboveground.

- **Terra Cotta.** Unglazed terra cotta is perhaps the most recognizable container garden vessel. Relatively tough, a clay pot is light enough to move by hand.

  Unglazed clay is porous. Raw clay soaks up water and allows the water to evaporate quickly through the pot, taking nutrient reserves with it. Always soak pots in water for a few hours just before planting to hydrate the clay. Use heavier soil mix, with a small percentage of perlite and vermiculite.

  Glazed terra cotta's exterior or overall finish seals the material and permits no water or air to pass, except through drain holes. Excessive watering and potential for fungal growth are the chief concerns. In cold, the glaze may flake off.

- **Stone and Concrete.** These containers are heavy and are best suited for ground-level planters. Stone and concrete are durable, provide above-average insulating value, and are adequately porous for nearly any plant or soil combination. Growth of moss and lichen on the outside of the container may add an attractive, weathered patina.

  Both may cause overly alkaline conditions. A limestone pot, for instance, can poison acid-loving plants. A popular remedy is to empty the pot, rinse it often, and let it weather in the rain until residual alkalinity has leached out of it.

- **Synthetics.** Plastic pots specifically are lightweight, durable, less-expensive alternatives that hold moisture and drain water adequately for almost any plant. Commonly molded to imitate terra-cotta pots, plastic maintains the look of new, unglazed clay for years while withstanding wear. Those reinforced with or made from fiberglass are frost resistant. In addition, synthetic containers can be assembled with integral watering systems, such as a section of drip irrigation tube that connects pot to pot.

In container gardening, size matters. In fact, the eventual size of a plant is arguably more important than the plant's shape, form, and proportion. Though its mature size is difficult to keep in mind—especially for beginning gardeners—when buying a young plant it's vital to know a plant's growth habit and its natural size and shape at maturity so that you can select an adequate container for its needs. Equally as important is what's going on under the soil in the development pattern of a plant's root system. Some species, such as azaleas, respond well to tight confines and, in fact, will slump if put in a vessel that is too large; most other plants prefer plenty of room to drink and get adequate nourishment from the water and nutrients in the soil.

A plant's shape and proportions—as it relates to its container, to other plants and their containers, and to the surrounding landscape and its structures—are design issues you also need to consider in creating an attractive, inviting garden setting. With potted plants available in so many forms, from conical trees to dome-shaped annuals and asymmetrical shrubs, not to mention trailers and climbers, it may take some experimentation to develop the right mix.

According to most good design edicts, start with a dominant or common plant shape to set the proportional base for your garden, then add contrasting and complementary forms and shapes to provide visual relief and interest.

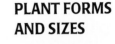

PLANT FORMS AND SIZES

(Above) What grows up isn't necessarily indicative of what grows down; be aware of a plant's root growth and eventual needs as you select its container.

The shape of the plant often determines the best shape for its container; notice how the cone-shaped tree and clipped shrub work best in narrow, cylindrical pots, while the two other plants would benefit more from smaller, squat containers that matched their growth habits.

SELECTING HEALTHY PLANTS

While your sense of style, available time, plant hardiness zone [see Appendix, pg. 131], and chosen containers will determine in large part your plant purchases, all your effort will be wasted unless you choose healthy specimens.

While that advice may seem obvious, it is even more critical with container gardens, where there is quite literally less room for plants to regain fitness if they're in poor shape already. Older plants may fill a large container right away, but they also are more set in their ways and may resist a smooth transfer or require a longer adjustment period. For this reason, it's best to select smaller, immature plants, which are able to bounce back more quickly from slight setbacks and repotting shock.

In most cases, roots hold the key to a plant's health. A rootbound plant is easy to distinguish. Simply examine the bottom of the pot and drain holes for signs of matted roots, and don't be shy about gently removing a small starter from its nursery container before making a purchase. For bare-root buys, look for a healthy, green tone, sturdy texture, and adequate separation among the roots.

Above ground, stems should be firm and easily bounce back if drawn down for inspection. The overall form of the plant should be well rounded and the leaves should be healthy. The foliage and flowers should be free of pests and signs of illness such as rust or mildew.

If a plant looks good on sight, with strong stems, bright flowers, and forming buds, that's a prime indication that its overall health is good.

Even the healthiest plants can fail, however, if placed in the wrong container. As you select your plants, make sure you know their watering and drainage needs, which will help determine the kind of pots—wood, glazed or unglazed terra cotta, metal, concrete, or plastic—that promote long-term health. It may be that your favorite plant just won't survive in your favorite container. In that case, consider planting in another, smaller vessel, then placing that container into your pot of choice.

Is it rootbound? Don't be shy about checking the root systems of plants before you buy them. Plants with overcrowded root systems may never recover or perform well, lessening your chance for success.

Of all the benefits of container gardening, the ability to easily manage and manipulate the soil tops the list. Most potting mixes are crumbly blends of organic matter, humus, and loam (an even blend of sand, silt, and clay); best is a good balance of all three. You can determine the relative content of these elements by how well the soil holds together when you firm it up in your fist. Generally, sandy soil will fall apart, while silty or clay-based soil will hold together. Sand in soil promotes drainage but is poor at retaining nutrients. A high clay or silt content, by contrast, retains nutrients but does not drain well.

The right balance of sand, clay, and silt depends on the needs of your plants at each stage of development. Compact soils that hold moisture longer are ideal for new shoots but are far less appropriate as plants mature. Heavier mixes often are recommended for larger trees and shrubs, especially those exposed to windy conditions, since they help anchor the root systems.

Most off-the-shelf potting mixes contain some nutrients—a balance of nitrogen, phosphorous, and potassium plus traces of other beneficial elements. Depending on the plants you select, however, it may be best to buy these nutrients separately and mix them in proper proportion to your plants' particular demands.

In containers, a balance of drainage, aeration (oxygen), and nutrients is the key to a soil mix that promotes healthy growth. Aeration and water retention may appear to be conflicting goals, but they are desirable in a container situation. A dose of compost, for instance, will help the soil retain moisture, while perlite (a volcanic mineral), sand, or peat moss can aid aeration.

As you peruse the potting-mix aisles, you'll notice two basic types of mixes: soil based and soilless. Soil-based mixes are derived from pasteurized garden loam, whereas soilless mixes combine peat, perlite, and vermiculite. Soil-based mixes are best suited for trees, shrubs, and other plants that require a reserve of nutrients in the soil. Soilless mixes are lighter and better for plants that require extra aeration.

Most prepared soil mixes are fine for the majority of potted plants, but non-natives and experimental varieties often require a custom mix of soil and organic (or synthetic) nutrients. Mixing your own soil helps ensure the greatest opportunity for success.

TOOLS AND MATERIALS

Whether you garden a lot or a little, chances are you already have some—or even all—of the basic tools needed for container gardening.

A basic set of hand tools includes a trowel or two, in rounded- and pointed-end styles, and a hand fork. Both will get a lot of use, so make sure you test the weight, balance, and comfort of the grip before you buy them. In addition to loosening and tamping soil, a hand fork is useful as a weeder.

Next, you'll need some pruning shears, preferably ones with a notch near the handle (or at the base of the blades) for cutting wire ties without damaging the cutting edges. Try several until you find a pair that feels comfortable in your hand; in addition, check the tension of the shears and the location and operation of the locking mechanism.

Last on the list is a heavy-duty watering can, though any size over a gallon or two (4–8 l) will provide you with a workout. Fit it with a bulb or rose diffuser to soften the flow of water. Use a pointed nozzle to direct water under foliage and to water only specific plants. Also consider a mister—perhaps just a hand-held spray bottle from the kitchen—to refresh and feed at leaf level. If your water source is nearby, using a garden hose is often faster and easier than carrying a can. A bubbler attachment is critical to control the flow and spray of a hose, while an extension, or boom, will allow you to reach hanging baskets and boxes without having to get the stepstool.

Plant foods and fertilizers, whether organic (above) or synthetic (top), are essential to the continued health of your potted plants, which cannot rely on open soil for needed nutrients and micronutrients.

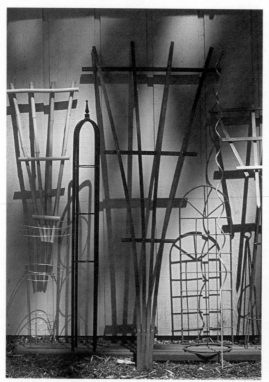

Your container gardening inventory may include vertical supports (right), whether premade or those of your own creation, to help direct and brace climbers and spreaders. In addition, potted plants require a variety of watering methods (far right), from simple cans to spout and hose attachments that diffuse the flow so soil and roots remain undisturbed.

SOURCES FOR PLANTS AND SUPPLIES

At one time the local nursery was the preferred place to purchase a variety of plants and seeds, fertilizer and soil, and containers and tools necessary for garden projects—and gain some good advice in the process. Today, choices abound. With the advent of retail garden centers, often as part of larger home-improvement outlets, the venues for plant selection, as well as access to expertise in care and maintenance, have increased dramatically. Even mass retailers now have first-rate garden sections.

The popularity of gardening also has generated an abundance of garden and flower shows, bringing with them a wider network of regional and national growers and seed companies and their wares, tempting you to try something non-native or exotic for your area.

Rapid advances in technology—including the electronic marketplace—have made the once-local garden club a global affair, allowing conversation between gardeners on virtually every part of the planet and permitting them to access the merchandise and specialized knowledge of seed and plant cataloguers, which usually offer a staggering array of plantings. In addition, many cataloguers are ahead of the curve on new varieties or strains of common plants, including hybrids—a particularly important consideration of container gardeners looking for dwarf or miniature versions of their favorite plants. Seeds purchased through a cataloguer sometimes may be fresher than those of local retailers, most of which stock their inventories a few months in advance of the season and may limit themselves to varieties suited to the demands, conditions, or trends of the local market.

Of course there's no substitute for the old standby: talking shop with an experienced neighbor over a fence. Gardeners love to swap stories as well as starters and seedlings, providing an equal dose of plants and advice in the process.

Nurseries and retail garden centers are one-stop shops for plants, soil, containers, and the rest of your gardening needs. Other sources include catalog and electronic-marketplace retailers—specialists for non-native plant varieties, as well as a continuing source of gardening tips and ideas.

CONTAINER GARDENING PLANNING FLOWCHART

A flowchart is a written checklist that allows you to quickly scan the major decisions that should be reviewed as you consider a garden project. The one illustrated here specifically deals with the decisions that gardeners must make when they undertake planting in containers. A few minutes spent with the checklist will ensure that you remember each waypoint to a successful project. Refer to the checklist before beginning a new planting—it will save you time and effort, including second trips to the garden store.

1 Site Choice Questions:
Where is your garden located, both geographically and within your yard or home? Is your proposed container garden located on a windowsill, roof deck, patio, entryway, or indoor room? What is its exposure to light and shade? What are the usual wind, temperature, and humidity conditions? Do you seek to visually enlarge the area, or make it more intimate? What types of containers will lend themselves to your planting and decorating choices, both practically and aesthetically?

DETERMINING YOUR OBJECTIVES

2 Goal Questions:
Why have you chosen to plant in containers? Is it for the ease of care, for the versatility of plantings, to enhance an outdoor space, or to garden in a small space? Do you want to experiment with non-native plantings or grow time-tested container plants that require little maintenance? Do you have containers in mind that will limit your choice of appropriate plantings, or does your selection of plants determine your containers?

PLANNING FOR THE PROJECT

ALLOCATING TIME AND SCHEDULING

3 Scale Questions:
Is your choice of container gardening for an indoor or outdoor space? Do you want your container garden to help define spaces, direct traffic, or provide a complementary color? How much time do you have available for planning, planting, and care? Will your project require special equipment or materials, and will you need assistance to complete it successfully? Can you complete the project in the time allotted?

4 **Plant Selection Questions:**
What are the growth habits, care needs, and color display features of the plants you desire? Do your chosen containers also meet those requirements? Does the care of your container plantings require that they be in moveable pots, to protect them from inclement weather or other adverse conditions? In the garden store, are seed racks complete and greengoods well maintained, healthy, and free of pests? Are plants of appropriate size available? How wide is the selection? Do the plants have adequate space for root growth? Is expert advice available? Are the containers solid and sound, with no cracks or other signs of wear, and clean and free of contamination?

PREPARING TO PURCHASE ANNUAL PLANTS

SOIL PREPARATION, MATERIALS, AND TOOLS

5 **Preparation Questions:**
Are your containers adequately prepared, including washing and sterilizing? Do they have adequate drainage holes? Have you selected soil mixes and fertilizers that match your plants' needs? What materials, supplies, tools, and gear will be required? Do you have the appropriate materials, including liners, hanging chains, and hardware for installing your container plantings safely? Should you install a fixed irrigation system? Have you planned for the size at maturity of your plantings, and the potential need for repotting?

FINDING HELP AND INFORMATION

6 **Resource and Aid Questions:**
Where will you turn for expert advice? Do you have current catalogs, periodicals, and books containing information about the plants and garden techniques you will require? Does your garden retailer have knowledgeable staff able to assist you in your decisions and answer questions? Have you identified your USDA plant hardiness zone and microclimate? Are you familiar with online electronic resources, or do you have access to your agricultural extension office agent? Are gardening classes available through educators in your area? Are there local experts who broadcast on radio or television to whom you may turn for questions and advice?

The Container Gardening Planning Flowchart [see pg. 24] is designed to give you a broader yet more focused perspective on your container planting options. Now that you've narrowed down your choices, it's time to prepare for planting, a step that includes evaluating sun and shade and adjusting for climate conditions.

Of course, unlike open gardens, container gardens also require the preparation of the containers themselves. A few of the most common and popular projects are building a plant post, installing a windowbox, building a raised bed, and constructing landscape and tree planters. In each case we provide full step-by-step instructions and accompanying photographs.

The first three projects require only minimal carpentry skills, a basic set of tools, and an afternoon's worth of time. Constructing landscape and tree planters is a bit more ambitious and thus may require more-advanced building skills (depending on the scope of your project, you may even need a building permit or other local approvals). Our step-by-step instructions will serve as building plans or, if you decide to hire professional help, a set of standards. Use them as a guide to selecting materials and planning the work.

At the conclusion of this chapter, you'll get ideas about how to optimize the effects of container planting indoors and outdoors, regardless of the size of your space.

> **From pots to plants, preparation is key for a successful container garden**

Preparing to Plant

Preparation is the key to achieving the effect you want in a container garden—which means first knowing the range of choices available and then selecting what's best for you and your situation.

INDOOR CONTAINER GARDENS

What used to be called "houseplants" have come a long way since the days when the term conjured up a low-maintenance ficus in a corner of the living room and a philodendron along an arched staircase shelf. Today's sophisticated indoor container gardens offer as much in function as they do in ornamental value.

Most new homes are designed with an "open" floor plan, which means that areas flow seamlessly into one another instead of being separated by walls, halls, and doorways. So popular is this interior design that removing such barriers in older homes has become a common remodeling project.

Container plants have taken on an important role in helping to define and enhance the functions of many indoor spaces. For example, three or four potted trees set in wicker baskets, which might normally frame a patio door, can be arranged easily to section off a portion of a great room, creating a more intimate space for dining.

Container plants can be used to direct traffic indoors, identifying the path you want guests to take through the house. Large plants can subtly block off private areas, such as the master bedroom or home office, during parties. Carefully chosen plants can shield from view a wall-mounted vent register (make sure the plants can handle the air flow) or hide stereo speakers without hindering their fidelity.

The range of indoor locations for container plants is as vast as, well, all outdoors: on the coffee table, buffet, or window seat; along the mantel; up the stairs; at the edge of a kitchen counter; draping the side of a cupboard; or hanging from both sides of an arched opening or alongside a doorway. The mobility of most potted plants allows them to be moved at whim—provided the new location has the necessary sun exposure.

Container plants placed along large picture windows or framing a sliding glass door leading to the backyard serve to blur the lines between indoors and out, visually expanding the space. Such locations are perfect for sun-loving species, which thrive on the solar gain from the glass.

Finally, the indoors often is the best place for edible treasures. A sunny window sill offers a nurturing environment for the plants—and easy access for the cook.

Indoor plants are useful, too—providing fresh herbs for a meal (above left), hiding stereo speakers (left), and allowing you to grow non-native species (top).

Although containers for outdoor plants are normally thought to be merely ornamental, in truth outdoor container plantings offer several practical functions. Contained plants can be used to define outdoor "rooms," lend privacy and shelter, and direct foot traffic. One of the least considered of their functional attributes is their ability to attract beneficial insects that feast on pests that feed on plants (such as ladybugs that eat aphids). Such natural pest-control measures [see Controlling Pests, pg. 74] add to the health of your plants and also preserve the natural order, sustaining the environment.

In the garden, though, function should be coupled with form, and the ability of container gardens to stimulate the senses and excite the eye must complement any utilitarian motives. Visual appeal must be weighed along with functionality.

Take a look around your yard, patio, or front stoop and identify areas that appear drab, monotonous, or just plain unsightly. Maybe the concrete steps leading up to an entry door have seen better days, or a white picket fence could use a refreshing jolt of color. Perhaps that hard-edged corner of the brick patio could use some softening provided by the rusticity of an oak barrel, or maybe there's a bare tree branch that could support a hanging basket or two.

Pathways leading to a covered porch or those alongside a house are especially suited to potted plants. A well-placed pot—or a grouping of them—can guide visitors to the party. When well chosen, a container of plants can soften the harsh lines of stepping stones or complement a soft walking path.

Entries to the house also benefit from potted plants. Stone urns, sprouting dwarf trees in a bed of stonecrop, can be a welcoming sentry, as can a tandem of hanging baskets flanking the back door.

Fasten an old letter box to one side of an entry and plant it with some daylilies, or hang a basket or box above a door with the chain leading up to a chime or bell. The key is to get creative.

OUTDOOR CONTAINER GARDENS

A potted plant's form is complemented by its function, whether adorning a garden pathway (top left) or beautifying and softening the edges of a concrete entryway (below).

EVALUATING SUN AND SHADE

Deciding what plants to purchase for a container—or where to place the container—depends on the pattern of sunlight and shadows it will receive. Light changes throughout a given day and from season to season.

To determine light conditions in your yard, patio, deck, or balcony, monitor the area a few times during the course of a day. Do this in spring or early summer, when most plants grow and bloom; observing in autumn or winter, when the sun is lower in the sky, will not provide an accurate gauge of the hours of sunlight your plantings will receive.

Step outside at about ten in the morning and take note of the areas of full sun, full shade, shadows, and filtered light created by tree branches or overhangs. Notice where the sun is in the sky. Then, around one in the afternoon, note the differences and similarities. At five in the afternoon, venture out for a final evaluation. Keep in mind that as the seasons progress, the angle of the sun rises and falls. Maintaining your notes for at least a week will allow you to project sunlight and shade exposures for at least three months out.

(Above) A photographic light meter can be an effective tool for comparing the relative amount of light in two different areas. Light exposure doubles with each increased step of f-stop. This information allows you to judge whether the sun exposure to your plantings is sufficient.

After you've evaluated the sun and shade patterns, you're ready to get your hands dirty—not planting, but picking up some soil in shady locations at ten, one, and five o'clock to see whether it is hot and dry or moist and cool. Determining how the soil texture in different areas of the yard changes during the day will inform your watering needs. Also observe the attributes of the surrounding air. Is the temperature in a shady spot markedly different from that of a sunny or speckled-light one? Most plants—even ivy, hostas, and most ferns—need at least a half-day of sunshine to grow well. Of course, that is a container advantage—you can move your garden to meet the needs of your plants.

Some plants, such as fern varieties (left), need shade to thrive. This allows you to fill the darker reaches of your garden with background color and texture. Others, such as annual flowers (right), need consistent sunlight to bloom and show off their colors. For both types of plantings, using mobile containers allows you to control the amount of sunlight and shade exposure they receive.

BUILDING A PLANT POST

Required Materials:

1	6-ft. (180-cm)	4×4 (89×89 mm)	Post
4	12-in. (30-cm)	1×8 (19×184 mm)	Shelves
2	18-in. (45-cm)	¾-in. (19-mm)	Dowel
1	Sack	Fence-post concrete mix	
1	Bottle	Woodworker's glue	
4	L-bracket shelf supports and fasteners		
1	1–qt. (1-l)	Paint	

Plant posts provide an attractive focal point in shady nooks or other background areas of the landscape. Because they raise potted plants and hanging baskets above the surrounding foliage, they appear framed by taller shrubs and the underfoliage of trees. Constructing and installing a plant post for your yard is a quick and simple project, requiring only a drill, a saw, and your time. Allow a couple of hours for construction and another for installing the post. Follow these easy instructions:

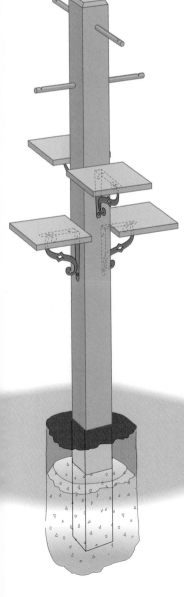

1 Drill two ¾-in. (19-mm) holes in the post, spaced 6 and 24 in. (15 and 60 cm) from the top of the post, on opposite faces.

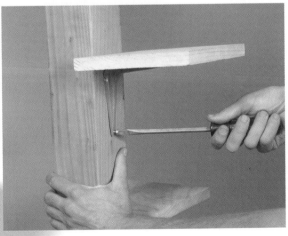

2 Thread the dowels through the post, gluing them into place when they are centered.

3 Install shelves to shelf brackets, then to post. Position each shelf 18 in. (45 cm) below the dowel above it. Prime the entire assembly prior to installation with exterior sealer or paint.

4 Dig a footing 18 in. (45 cm) deep, then level and brace the post and fill with concrete.

PLANTING IN DRY CLIMATES

So you live in an arid climate—what about you? Whether it's a desert where even shady spots are parched, or a plain where you almost can see the wind sapping moisture from the ground, you still can plant a thriving container garden.

Xeriscaping, which was developed as a water-conservation method in the 1970s, promotes the use of drought-resistant plants native to dry climates. This, in turn, has spawned interest in a wide variety of plants, including trees, shrubs, grasses, and flowers, that adapt well or are naturally comfortable in dry conditions. (Because most plants in containers are more apt to experience drought than those planted in open ground, they also are a perfect choice for gardeners in moist or wet climates.)

Remember, though, that even genetically drought-tolerant plants are susceptible to water stress. They will show the typical symptoms of thirst—from withering foliage to disease—if watered frequently at first and then deprived of water. On the other hand, if water is rationed early on, then applied judiciously, these plants will adapt and thrive.

If you have your heart set on adding unique texture or color to your garden by nurturing non-native species that are shade and moisture lovers, planting them in containers is likely your only option. Installing a drip irrigation system to keep them well watered, and

(Above) Plants that are native to arid or hot climates already have adapted to lack of water and are thus well suited to containers.

planting them in moveable pots so that you can shade them from the heat of the day, are two steps toward success.

Applying organic mulches, including peat moss, manure, and compost, will help retain moisture in a container's soil, provide nutrients, and generally maintain good plant health. Inorganic mulches, such as perlite or sand, when well watered in, add no nutrients but are effective in slowing drainage.

The pots you use also will have an impact on moisture retention. Unglazed terra cotta, for instance, is highly evaporative, as are wire-mesh hanging baskets. Conversely, glazed terra cotta and wood retain moisture better. Keep this in mind when choosing your containers, plantings, and means of delivering water.

(Right) A drip irrigation system is an effective way to keep potted plants adequately watered, regardless of climate or season. Some even can be equipped with sensors that provide watering only when the plant needs it.

INSTALLING SPRINKLERS IN CONTAINERS

Watering container gardens is easily automated through installation of a simple drip irrigation system, comprising a battery-operated timer valve attached to your hose bib faucet, supply tubing or pipe, and drip emitter fixtures [see A Simple Drip System, pg. 47]. Once your system is in place, install a drip emitter to feed water into each container. Emitters are available in a range of dispersal patterns and flow rates. Follow these instructions for watering fixed planters:

1 Cut ½-in (10-mm) PVC pipe to length depending on your site, using plastic pipe cutters to ensure a clean, smooth cut.

2 At each container, prime the pipe and a slip-to-thread "street el" fitting, then apply waterproof solvent glue. Twist the connection 90° as you join the pieces to ensure a good fit. Allow the joint to dry completely before pressurizing the line.

3 To each street el attach a cutoff riser, then a drip manifold fixture. They come in 2-, 4-, and 6-outlet models and feed ¼-in (6-mm) drip tube.

4 Using a masonry drill, create a hole in the bottom of the catch basin and container, and feed the water supply tube into the container.

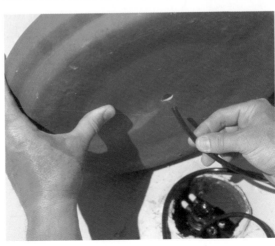

5 After planting the container, attach a drip emitter to the supply tube and set it in place using a plastic stake to secure it.

OPTIMIZING SMALL SPACES

Many people think placing a container garden in a small space will make the space appear smaller. In fact, arranging items vertically makes an area seem more open (think of closet organizers). This design principle holds true whether you are planning a container garden for indoors or outdoors. Consider these ideas:

- Hook hanging baskets to walls and along the rim of a porch, patio, or balcony roof overhang. Choose plants that either drape down or climb the cable support. Make sure the structure can support the weight of the potted plant, and use recommended fasteners. Also, make sure that water drains away from high-traffic areas.

- Hang shallow, lightweight boxes under windows and along deck and porch railings to soften the sharp lines of those areas. On railings, consider boxes that hook onto or strap over the top of the balustrade, providing more-secure connections than screws or nails.

- Fill a corner, front a blank wall, or enclose an outdoor area on one side with a lattice or an arbor, then plant climbing flowers and other plants with vertical-growth habits to cover it.

- Use smaller pots in greater numbers instead of just a few big ones. Smaller containers are easier to move and rearrange; cluster them in one area to focus the effect, or spread them out to enclose and define a space.

- If you like big containers, use them to plant trees or shrubs with tall foliage—they can fill a blank corner, provide a backdrop for smaller containers, or help focus the eye on key features.

- Hang baskets from low-growing tree limbs, fence posts, slats, and gates. To protect the health of trees and the structural integrity of fence or gate components, feed hanging straps through a length of discarded garden hose instead of using nails to secure the containers.

- Build a tiered or multilevel structure for your containers; this will achieve the same effect as displaying them by other vertical means. In addition to the traditional "pyramid" shape, consider the inverted pyramid, "twin peaks," or other creative arrangements.

Think vertical—especially when space is tight. Consider the height of the plant at maturity, the size of the container's base and its total weight, how pruning and training can keep the plant growing upward (drawing the eye with it), and fitting the container to its footprint on the ground.

PLANTING A WINDOWBOX

Seasonal color can highlight the architectural features of your home, a job tailor-made for annuals. Filling windowboxes with growing flowers takes only a few hours of planning, purchasing, and installation. Choose annuals that either trail over the edge or mound high up into the window opening, where they appear as though in a frame. Follow these easy steps for perfect results:

2 If access is limited, install a timed drip irrigation line to each pot [see Installing Sprinklers in Containers, pg. 33].

1 Measure the dimensions and depth of the windowbox, and purchase weatherproof containers sized to fit snugly within the box.

3 Plant annuals into the containers, using a pair of transplants in each pot (this avoids gaps in the floral display if one plant should fail). Add a whimsical garden decoration, if desired.

4 Annuals grow quickly, filling the windowbox with color. Remember that pot plantings should be fertilized every other week throughout the growing season.

RAISED BEDS

A European invention formally introduced to the United States in the mid-1960s, the practice of gardening in raised beds has since grown in popularity and creativity to produce small-scale, highly productive vegetable gardens; easy-to-manage perennial plots; and almost any other kind of home you can imagine for nearly any kind of plantings. They are the secret to achieving a thriving flower display.

Especially appropriate for areas with difficult native soil conditions, such as heavy sand or clay content, raised beds allow you to mix your own soil or use a premixed potting formula. Like containers, the beds themselves can be a showcase and focal point of a garden, while the ability to manipulate the soil content affords the opportunity to try non-native plants or experiment with combinations of color and texture that would be difficult to achieve in an open bed.

Raised beds can be constructed on flat plots or slopes in whatever size and dimension your site allows. They often are created for community gardens and retirement villages to accommodate gardeners of varying ages and abilities. Children, the elderly, and folks with limited mobility, for instance, benefit from the easier access to plants, flowers, and vegetables offered by raised beds.

Building raised beds is a fairly simple process, requiring basic carpentry skills and common materials and tools. The key is to build a stable box that will hold soil and retain moisture while providing drainage. For those reasons, wood is the most popular raised-bed material, though rigid plastic components also will do the job.

Raised beds combine the best of both open and contained gardens: plants are given more room to develop their root systems, while you maintain control over such critical elements as soil content, water, and nutrients.

BUILDING A RAISED BED

Required Materials:

4	2×12-in. (38×286-mm)	Side boards
	(Dimension as required for site and project)	
12	3/8×3 1/2-in. (10×90-mm)	Deck screws
12	1-in. (25-mm)	Flat washers

Raised-bed gardens have become a fixture of many home landscapes. Simple in concept and installation, raised beds are open-bottom frames that hold rich, fertile soil above the surrounding grade. Use pressure-treated lumber for durable flower beds, but never for vegetable plantings—avoid potential hazard from poisoning. Installing a raised bed is a 6–8-hour project. Follow these steps for a great-looking bed:

1 Mark the outline of the bed, then level and excavate the area within the future bed to a depth of 6 in. (15 cm).

2 Using a power drill fitted with a 1/4-in. (6mm) bit, predrill three holes at each corner junction. Thread a washer onto each deck screw and fasten the corners, using a socket wrench.

3 Fill the planter with amended soil, replacing all native soil. Level and rake the bed.

4 Plant the finished bed, watering thoroughly to settle and firm the imported soil used to fill the planter.

LANDSCAPE PLANTERS

If you have the space and want better control over the soil mix surrounding your trees and shrubs, structural landscape planters are the perfect hybrid between a container garden and open ground.

Most basic construction materials are appropriate for landscape containers, including wood, stone, brick, and concrete masonry units (blocks or CMUs). The choice depends on your skills and budget as well as the look of the finished planter in relation to the rest of your garden's landscape features. For instance, if you have a flagstone path, a matching veneer on a concrete masonry planter would provide a nice complement; similarly, a redwood or cedar container could echo a raised deck constructed of the same material, as would an attractive brick planter built in front of a home constructed of matching brick.

Compared to raised beds, however, building a structural landscape planter requires a bit more skill in a variety of construction methods and materials [see opposite]. These include a basic understanding of concrete masonry for building forms, installing reinforcement rod and pouring the footing; methods of concrete-block wall construction using mortar and preformed block units; and possibly applying stucco or attaching facings and stone to enhance the outer appearance of the planter.

Most basic construction materials are appropriate for landscape planters. Matching the material to the home's facade—in this case, traditional brick—gives the entire property a unified appearance while defining discrete areas.

If you lack the necessary skills to do it yourself, many building contractors can help you design and complete your project. Regardless of whether you construct the planter personally or hire a tradesman, a good understanding of the steps employed will help inform your decisions and keep expenses low.

A concrete-block planter affords you a lot of flexibility in finishes. It can be left as is, especially if it features a textured face. It also can be finished in stucco or a thin layer of smooth or textured masonry. Veneer finishes, such as stone or brick, add dimensionality and help match other architectural features in your landscape or yard.

When choosing plants or trees for an existing landscape planter, or for one that you are constructing, determine their size at maturity to avoid damage to the plant and the planter.

CONSTRUCTING A LANDSCAPE PLANTER

Structural planters are large, permanent landscape fixtures at the extreme end of container gardening. Use them to define walkways, to create a focal point for your yard, or for other design purposes. Building a planter requires several weeks of planning and work, following these general steps:

1 Carefully mark the site and build forms for the footing. It should be at least 6 in. (15 cm) deep and 12 in. (30 cm) wide.

4 Installing a large tree—here, a 5-ft.-tall (1.5-m) box-specimen maple—into the partially completed planter requires rental of heavy-lifting equipment or contracting with a tree-moving specialist. Install smaller plants using the same methods as for your other container plantings.

2 Pour concrete into the form, leveling and steel troweling the surface as it dries, to obtain a flat surface for block construction.

3 Apply concrete bond mixture to the footing, then set construction blocks in mortar around the perimeter to create the planter's sidewall, reinforcing with rebar.

5 For a more attractive planter, face the block wall with brick or synthetic stone fastened with mortar.

Gardening is a little like painting your house: doing it right requires a lot of preparation, followed by the fun of actually painting—and, of course, is enormously rewarding. The container gardening equivalent of selecting your paint, sanding any rough edges, and applying the primer coat is choosing your plantings, preparing the container, and mixing in the right soil and amendments.

Proper preparation will deliver the desired effect for your garden and make care and maintenance chores easier and more effective. For instance, the containers you select, whether they're new or recycled, may need special preparation or treatment depending on their condition and the plantings you've chosen; they also may require accessories, such as stands and rollers. Finally, the plants you choose to put in them will require the correct soil mix and fertilizers—perhaps even a dedicated watering system—to realize your container gardening goal.

Proper preparation is all that's needed for a container to support any type of plant

Planting in Containers

This chapter provides the basics of proper preparation for many different types of container plantings, from vegetables and fruits to shrubs, trees, ferns, roses, and grasses. You'll get tips for achieving dramatic annual and perennial color, as well as the basics necessary for creating a water garden and installing vertical supports for your climbers and vines. Equipped with this information, you'll be ready to move on to the best part of container gardening—planting.

Regardless of your choice of plants, comprehensive and proper preparation is the basis of successful container gardening.

PREPARING CONTAINERS FOR PLANTING

W hether your choice of container is a terra-cotta pot or a whimsical work boot, it must be able to hold enough soil, provide adequate drainage, and otherwise ensure the health of the plantings it contains.

The first and most important need of any container is that it be cleaned and conditioned. Even new pots, especially those made from synthetic materials, may contain some chemical residue; just sitting out in the yard, nursery, or garden center invites dust, dirt, old root stems, and other potential hazards to settle in.

Immerse the container in cold, clean water for a few hours to loosen up any debris, then scrub it inside and out with a stiff brush and some liquid detergent. Apply a mild bleach solution [see Sterilizing Containers, below] to rid the container of any fungus spores or latent bacterial infection. Finally, dunk the container in clean water to wash off any residue from the cleansers. Remember to use this same process on gravel or bits of broken clay pots used as drainage media.

Long-term durability is a valuable convenience, relieving you from repotting should a vessel fail. With any container, whether new or old, check for cracking, chipping, flaking, and other signs of damage or wear that might cause failure and require replanting.

Most pots manufactured as planters include integral drain holes in the bottom or sides, but those that are handmade or recycled from another use probably will need to have a few drain openings added. The easiest method for making drainage holes is to use an electric drill fitted with a sharp carbide metal bit measuring about ⅝ inch (16 mm) in diameter. To avoid cracking or breaking the container, apply masking tape where you want to drill the holes, and practice on a scrap piece first.

Drainage holes need to be kept clean and clear to do their job. For almost all potted plants, "crocking" is a way to promote proper drainage and also keep pests from entering. To crock a container, secure a section of thin zinc gauze or fine stainless wire mesh over each hole on the inside of the pot, then cover with a drainage medium, such as bits of a broken terra-cotta pot (laid with the curvature up), washed granite pebbles, or other neutral aggregate. This layer filters out debris, fine soil, and sand that can silt or clog the drain holes and waterlog the plant's roots.

Warning

Household bleach contains sodium hypochlorite, a powerful skin and eye irritant. Avoid hazard by wearing gloves and protecting clothing whenever mixing or pouring bleach solution.

STERILIZING CONTAINERS

1 Fill a clean 2-gal. (7.6-l) bucket with tap water and ½ cup (125 ml) of bleach; protect your hands by wearing gloves.

2 Gently wash the entire container, removing any dirt inside and out, then gently scrub in bleach solution. Rinse in clean water.

WATERPROOFING CONTAINERS

Because of their porosity, unglazed terra-cotta and wood pots are especially susceptible to water damage from wet soil and evaporation through the container. To maintain their viability as adequate planters, they can easily be waterproofed on their inside surfaces with common water-resistant compounds. One caveat: altering the porosity of a container also means altering your watering schedule for the plant it holds.

1 Get ready for work with protective gloves, a drop cloth, a paintbrush, and latex waterproofing compound (available from garden and hobby stores). Make sure the container is clean and free of any dirt or debris.

2 Treat only the inside surface. Apply compound evenly (avoid top-to-bottom brush strokes); instead, overlap horizontal strokes to ensure a complete seal.

3 Pour excess waterproofing solution back into its container (assuming the pot was first cleaned and the compound is uncontaminated).

3 Invert the sterilized container on a drying rack. Allow the container to dry completely before planting.

HANGING CONTAINER GARDENS

One of the many virtues of hanging baskets is that they can be planted year-round, providing blooming sentries for an entry, lining the eaves of a covered porch, or brightening an arbor or gazebo. Perhaps best of all, they are simple to create and, with the right choice of plantings, equally simple to maintain.

Several types of hanging planters are available. One of the most popular is the open-wire variety, consisting of medium-gauge metal mesh that allows wide gaps for trailers through the bottom and along the sides. While tastes in plantings differ, most gardeners who plant in hanging baskets select foliage and flowers, such as lobelia or dusty miller, that provide lasting color and texture. The plantings eventually obscure the container, climbing over and draping down from it.

Because hanging baskets are exposed on all sides, they need some special care. For example, the porosity of an open mesh basket tends to dry out the soil and plants quickly, especially when it is in a sunny site and subject to summer breezes. Since proper drainage is essential, the regular discharge can slicken or stain the surface below. Also, the combined weight of the container, soil, plants, and water requires careful consideration of placement and secure supports and fastening.

Once you've finished creating your basic planting, you can fill in the rest of the basket with a wide variety of annuals and perennials, adding more soil as you go. Petunias and impatiens are popular and well suited to hanging baskets, as are climbers such as ivy-leaved geraniums, which will cover the hanging chain. Whichever combination of plantings you choose, keep in mind their varying bloom times and hardiness [see Encyclopedia of Container Plants, pg. 97]. That way, you'll always have a lush garden.

The variety of hanging container plants—from climbers to trailers—can occupy a generous amount of vertical space, effectively bringing your garden off the ground and up to eye level.

PLANTING HANGING BASKETS

Creating a garden in a hanging container is quite similar to planting in any other vessel you might choose. Some hanging containers are closed and sealed, while others are open—allowing you to add sphagnum moss to create a "living" basket.

1 As with any project, assemble your materials before you begin, including the proper soil mix, sphagnum moss, plants, a thin sheet of plastic or basket liner, and the container itself—here, an open wire variety, complete with a hanging chain and sturdy fasteners.

2 Dampen the moss and line the frame with it, then add a layer of plastic sheet, hiding its edges. To insert plants through the body of the container, make small slits in the plastic.

3 Add soil mix atop the plastic, filling the container nearly to the top. Firm the soil by pressing down with the flat of your palms.

4 Open the soil with your hands to accommodate the plants. Set trailers around the outside, tall bushes in the center. Select plants with similar root growth to avoid crowding.

AUTOMATIC WATERING SYSTEMS

As a watering method, a drip irrigation system's appeal extends beyond those gardeners who lack time—indeed, it's the ultimate testament to a gardener's commitment. Automated watering systems arguably are the best way to deliver and control the amount of water that container plants need, as well as where and when they need it. The fact that such a system makes your job a little easier also means that you will have more free time to plant, prune, and propagate your garden.

The basic elements of a drip irrigation system are shown opposite. The main line typically comes in the same sizes and lengths as standard garden hoses; manufacturers rate supply lines according to the number of emitters they can support while effectively serving a given number of plants. The drip tubing that runs between supply and emitter also is rated for the volume of water it can carry; plan on installing a single tube for every ten container plants served by the system.

In addition to these main components, there are a bevy of accessories and add-on features worthy of consideration. Main lines can be fitted with emitters—misters, bubblers, or sprayers. Misters are ideal for plants that benefit from moisture through their leaves, bubblers gurgle at the root line, and sprayers distribute water from a quarter-circle to a half-circle, at low or high pressure. All emitters are flow rated, allowing the gardener to determine the timing needed for adequate watering.

Regardless of the type of system you use, keep in mind that you'll need to keep a watchful eye on whether your plants are getting a proper dose of water at the right time. If close monitoring isn't practical, consider adding sensors that measure the soil's moisture content and signal the system to turn off and on as needed.

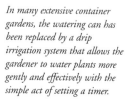

In many extensive container gardens, the watering can has been replaced by a drip irrigation system that allows the gardener to water plants more gently and effectively with the simple act of setting a timer.

A SIMPLE DRIP SYSTEM

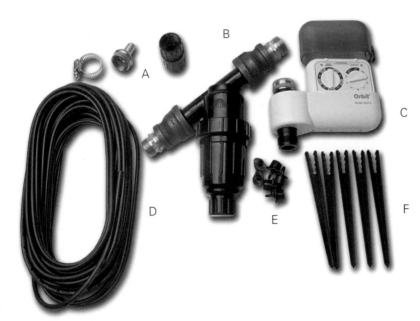

Create drip systems quickly and inexpensively by attaching battery-controlled timers and filters to nearby faucets or hose bibs. Drip irrigation conserves by emitting a flow of water to each plant. A single system can water up to 30 plants, depending on your water pressure. Follow these steps:

Required Components:

A Couplers and fittings
B Drip irrigation water filter
C Battery-timed hose-bib irrigation valve
D Drip irrigation line hose
E Drip emitters
F Line-placement stakes

1 Couple timer valve to hose bib, then install an in-line water filter to prevent clogged lines. Bushings may be needed where threads do not match exactly.

2 From the filter, attach the drip supply hose. This large-diameter hose carries pressurized water to the attachment points on each drip line. It may have several joints and junctions, depending on your garden.

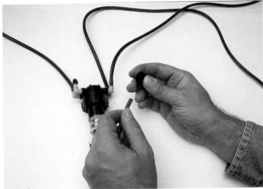

3 Wherever a drip line is needed, terminate the supply hose with a drip-line coupler, available in 2-, 4-, and 8-connection models. Attach ¼-in. (6-mm) supply tubing and one or more emitters.

VERTICAL SUPPORTS

Acontainer garden that draws the eye upward, shields a dismal view, or adorns a blank wall also provides a palette of color and texture. These upwardly mobile plants set in containers may require a little help from their friends.

The basic component of vertical support is the stake or cane, a thin, dowellike pole that bolsters sprawling or immature plants that cannot support their own weight or that are subject to high-wind conditions. Multiple stakes also can be attached to strings or wires, encouraging climbers such as jasmine and tendril growers such as sweet pea to latch on and leverage themselves up.

Tying a plant to a vertical support requires a deft touch and a stretchy, insulated tie that won't cut through or otherwise damage the plant's stem as it grows. Fasten ties loosely to allow the plant to move.

When placing stakes or canes, make sure they are as tall as the mature height of the plant being supported. Place stakes or canes in the soil before you plant to avoid damaging the roots. Once the plant begins to grow and lean toward the sun, droop under its own weight, or become subject to the wind, gently tether it to the support with plastic-coated wire or uncoated string.

Climbers with heavy foliage may need even more stability in the form of a trellis [see Installing Plant Supports, opposite], usually made from thin pieces of treated wood. Like most supports, a trellis provides the basic framework for a climbing plant's growth and spread. The design and dimension of your trellis, therefore, should be constructed to allow for a plant's growth patterns as well as the ultimate shape you want the plant to assume.

Set your trellis inside a long wooden planter alongside a house wall, fence, or garage. Place it 3 inches (8 cm) away from the surface to allow air to circulate behind it and to avoid excessive drying of flowers and foliage due to reflected heat.

Arbors, gazebos, and structures covering decks or other outdoor areas also provide the opportunity to train and support climbing container plants. Make sure the structure is latticed or otherwise allows air circulation, unless you intend to cultivate hardy climbers such as ivy.

For young climbers and vines, a simple mat of crumpled wire cloth is a great way to get the plant started and direct its ultimate shape and foliage development.

INSTALLING PLANT SUPPORTS

Support your climbers with a trellis attached to the back face of your planter. Trellises and other supports can be purchased premade or constructed in your own workshop; commonly, they are just sections of square or lattice slats nailed or stapled together to form a simple grid. If you choose to build a trellis yourself, make sure it has long enough "legs" to reach into the full depth of the planter.

1 Fill the planter with potting soil, compacted slightly to achieve the desired quantity, texture, and density.

2 Fit the trellis extensions into the soil along the back edge of the planter; compact the soil around them. Fasten the legs to the planter with screws or nails for added stability.

3 Wind the vines or limbs of your plant through a few of the trellis openings, guiding the growth onto the trellis.

4 Loosely tie the ends of the vines or limbs to the trellis structure as they develop new runners and growth.

5 Your trellis planter will create a wall of flowers and foliage that grow at eye level.

CREATING A SIMPLE WATER GARDEN

Constructing a water garden is easier than it might seem, though to be sure, only specialized plants are appropriate for it. These are aquatic plants—such as dwarf varieties of cattails, bulrushes, and water lilies—that require boggy moisture. In addition, water garden plants must be set in specially formulated aquatic soil and topdressed with a layer of washed gravel to filter the water, help control its flow into the pots, and add necessary weight to hold them at their submerged levels.

It's best to plant aquatic plants such as water lilies (a blooming perennial) in late spring. This allows their broad leaves to grow and cover most of the water's surface, protecting their roots from the sun's heat and limiting the spread of water algae (which is less likely to grow when plant leaves block the water from excessive sunlight).

Other plants, such as cattails, some grasses, and trailers such as parrot feather, can add dimension, texture, and unique colors to your container garden and are easy to maintain. Generally, water plants thrive in partial sun; they should be kept clear of falling leaves and other debris from overhead foliage.

In addition to using the right plants and soil, the only other major consideration is that the main container be completely watertight and large enough to hold at least 25 gallons (100 l) of water. For non-watertight vessels, consider setting a smaller, leak-proof container inside your favorite planter.

Once the potted plants are positioned, gently and slowly fill the pond or basin with water from a garden hose. If you plan to add fish, before introducing them to your water garden ask for expert advice at the store where you purchase them on how to condition the water properly.

Though it looks natural, this water garden is man-made with plants that either require constant moisture or can survive underwater. They are planted in special aquatic soils held in submerged, weighted containers.

Water ponds with aquatic plants provide an excellent focal point for pathside areas with filtered sunlight or complete shade. Follow the step-by-step instructions shown opposite to build the pond featured here using readily available materials.

BUILDING AN AQUATIC GARDEN

Water gardens look spectacular, add a special element to any garden, and can be created easily using materials and plants that are readily available. Building the garden requires a bit more skill than potting a petunia, but the effort is well worth it and boasts major paybacks in satisfaction. Follow these steps for a successful project:

2 Insert the premolded liner into the hole. Use a straightedge and level to check the installation.

1 Dig and level a hole of the desired shape and depth; premolded plastic pond liners are available in a variety of popular shapes. Make sure you set the pond or tub on a level base of builder's sand.

3 Fill the liner with water to bed it securely in the sand. Frame the top edge of the basin with river rock or other stone. Dry stack the stones in a double-height row to create the desired appearance.

4 Fill the pond with tap water and insert a special aquatic filter (similar to a fish-tank filter) to aerate and keep the water fresh; hide or bury the filter's supply-line hose beneath the stones.

5 Plant aquatic plants in a mix of potting soil and sand, topped with a 1-in. (25-mm) layer of coarse pea gravel. Weight the pots and settle them slowly into the pond.

PLANTING ANNUALS FOR COLOR

Even though annuals are single-season plants, not all of them bloom at the same time. Use this to your advantage: with proper planning and plant selection, you can enjoy annuals' color from late spring to late autumn by creating a changing palette of colors and foliage texture using container plantings.

Many annuals are inexpensive, fast blooming, and easy to manage in containers. To plant a succession of flowering annuals that will last a full season (and, depending on your climate, perhaps year-round), use both hardy, or cool-season, annuals and half-hardy, or warm-season, varieties. Start with cool-season annuals planted in early spring to bloom within six weeks or so. As days grow longer and the sun beats down in midsummer, replace the cool-season plants with half-hardy annuals. In late summer or autumn, once again plant cool-season annuals.

The blooming period for both hardy and half-hardy annuals can be extended and enhanced through the practice of deadheading. Once the flowers on a stem begin to wilt and die, pinch off the seedheads to allow the plant to focus its full energy on new flower production.

As with any plant, the eventual size and growth habits of your annuals should dictate the size of the container. At minimum, the pot needs to be 6 inches (15 cm) deep, more so for multiple plants; those flowers expected to grow a foot (30 cm) or more need a container width of at least 8 inches (20 cm). A great advantage of annuals is that you typically can plant them within 4 inches (10 cm) of each other because their roots won't compete.

To ensure success in containers, select healthy starts—those with well-developed roots, robust green stems and leaves, and compact, strong growth. Clean the container thoroughly [See Preparing Containers for Planting, pg. 42] and use fresh potting soil. To alleviate conflicting watering, feeding, and shade requirements among several varieties in the same container, consider an arrangement of smaller, single-plant pots.

As with open garden beds, annuals in containers bring dramatic seasonal color to the garden; unlike bedded plants, however, potted flowers can be moved and rearranged to create a variety of effects within the entire landscape.

Annuals are perhaps the simplest plants to pot, with starter kits and medium-texture potting soil readily available at nurseries, home, and garden centers.

PLANTING ANNUALS IN CONTAINERS

The great thing about annuals is that they look terrific as blooming nursery starts and only get better as they fill out and continue their bloom throughout the season. Planting them is easy, especially given how quickly they make their dramatic impact on the garden. Follow these simple steps:

2 Gently compact the soil, adding as needed to reach 1–2 in. (25–50 mm) below the rim of the container.

3 Carefully ease your starts out of their nursery containers and gently loosen the soil around the roots with a hand fork, breaking up any roots that encircle the rootball.

1 Select and fill your planter with a medium-texture bedding soil or potting mix.

4 With a trowel, dig planting holes large enough for the roots of the starts. Leave a space between plants to allow for root and plant growth.

5 Compact the potting mix around each rootball; add more soil as necessary to cover the roots completely and stabilize the plants. Water immediately after planting.

PLANTING PERENNIAL FLOWERS

By definition, perennials last year after year, providing colorful flowers throughout the season and healthy foliage throughout most of the year. Properly maintained in a suitable climate, they will flourish in containers for five years or more before you will have to move them into open soil.

Unlike annuals and bulbs, the roots of most perennials spread wide and deep. In a container, this proclivity requires a watchful eye and a commitment to pruning, repotting, and dividing to control growth and give the plant proper room to thrive. For this reason, no more than two perennials usually share a container. If your heart is set on multiple perennials, choose a pot that's at least 24 inches (60 cm) in diameter, and expect to repot or divide your plants every year or two.

By their second year, most blooming perennials burst with color that can last weeks or even months. Prune back the plant just after its bloom to promote more prolific and compact blooms in subsequent years.

Unlike plants in an open garden, potted perennials won't survive severe cold and must be protected (or overwintered) during dormant months to defend their root systems and latent buds. A cool space is best, and even a deep, covered porch close to the house may be adequate in mild-winter climates. Remember to water dormant plants during winter.

Dormancy is the best time to repot. Divide the root masses into smaller clumps. Use standard potting mix with a good dose of sand and perlite to help drainage.

Planting perennials requires vision beyond a single season, including choosing a container size and placement that will allow the plant to mature properly and have room for its foliage and roots.

Select a container about twice the size of the nursery pot, keeping in mind that, with proper care, a healthy and maturing perennial likely will need transplanting at midseason to provide it necessary room for root growth—then require transplanting again in the second year.

PLANTING PERENNIALS IN CONTAINERS

Unlike annuals, perennials have extensive root systems that require protection and care during transplanting. Healthy plants will be on the verge of outgrowing their nursery vessel and will welcome the elbow room afforded by a new, larger container. Transplant perennials by following these steps:

2 With your hands, mold soil to the container sides, creating a bowl for the plant's deepest roots.

1 Select and clean your container. Cover its drain hole with wire mesh and fine gravel or other drainage medium. Add about 3 in. (75 mm) of moist potting soil, to cover the bottom.

3 Invert and gently ease your plant out of its nursery container. Avoid using a trowel to loosen the plant, as you might damage sensitive roots.

4 Loosen the rootball where roots are matted or encircle the plant. Place the plant in the new container with the top of its rootball slightly above the soil surface and just below the container's rim.

5 Backfill the container with potting soil. Compact the soil gently to stabilize it. Leave the top of the rootball slightly exposed, with the plant at its original level.

PLANTING VEGETABLES

There's nothing quite like the flavor of freshly picked produce, which is why many flower gardeners hold vegetable gardeners in high esteem, assuming that growing edibles is a job only for the most skilled and diligent. Growing nutritious vegetables in containers actually requires the same skills as those used for other potted plants.

Planting edibles in containers also offers some key advantages over open vegetable gardens. You can provide the ideal soil mix for the vegetables and better manage root competition. Soil warms more quickly in containers, so even those maintained outdoors will get off to a good start as soon as temperatures warm. Exposure to sun and shade also is managed much more easily with moveable pots.

Given the higher level of control in a contained garden, your crop choices are almost limitless; however, certain varieties adapt better than others to being in a pot. Shallow-rooted plants, for instance, can be grouped in the same vessel, especially if they are thinned out during harvest to avoid crowding.

Other common container vegetables are the compact or baby-sized varieties of carrots, tomatoes, peppers, potatoes, and onions; increasingly, you can find cultivars especially created for container cultivation, which provide yields similar in volume, if not size, to those from open gardens.

Most vegetables thrive in direct sunlight. In early season, they need at least six hours of sun a day; by midsummer, however, a few may require some shading to prevent them from "bolting"— producing flowering heads that deliver no produce.

Fertilizers and nutrients are essential components of any successful vegetable garden but often require a more delicate touch when applying to container plants. A generous amount of slow-release, organic fertilizer mixed in with the soil, with a boost every third week, is best for promoting steady and healthy growth.

Because container soil can dry out more quickly than soil in an open garden, potted plants need regular watering. Subject to wilt, vegetables have a hard time recovering and will deliver less produce. Soil generally should be kept moist 1–2 inches (25–50 mm) from the surface but allowed to nearly dry out before another watering.

To plant a single plant in a pot, choose a container at least 12 inches (30 cm) deep—more for multiple plantings —to allow adequate room for root development. This shallow dimension accommodates a wide assortment of container choices, from hanging baskets trailing with tomatoes to long, narrow planters.

Potted vegetables add color and texture to your container garden, while yielding produce in close proximity to the kitchen.

It may look strange as a seedling, but eventually this tomato plant will engulf its support, yielding a season's worth of bounty in the form of tasty, fragrant fruit.

PLANTING CONTAINER TOMATOES

Vegetable plants, especially tomatoes, beans, and squash, grow and mature to large sizes. They always require support to accommodate their growth and keep their yield of produce within easy reach. With potted vegetables, it's often best to select dwarf varieties of your favorites—they require less room as they mature. Follow these steps for planting a tomato vine, a vegetable gardener's favorite:

1 Along with your seedling or nursery start, gather your materials—here a container, potting soil, and a pair of arched bamboo supports— to brace the maturing plant.

2 Place wire screen and drainage medium over the container's drain hole. Fill with potting mix until nearly full, then compact the soil.

3 With a trowel, create space in the soil for your seedling deep enough to accommodate its roots and the first two pairs of true leaves.

4 Invert and tap to ease the seedling out of its existing container. Set the plant into the hole, burying it to cover its rootball, lower stem, and bottom leaves. The buried leaves will sprout roots, adding to the plant's vigor.

5 Lightly compact the soil around the stem. Insert the vertical supports perpendicular to each other, forming an X at the top where they join [see photo opposite].

PLANTING HERBS

With their many attributes—including lengthy growth for many seasons, compact roots and foliage, typically high yield, and low maintenance requirements—herbs are perfectly suited for life in containers. (A brief list of common herbs can be found in the Encyclopedia of Container Plants [see pg. 123].)

Like many annuals, perennials, biennials, and even evergreen shrubs, herbs can grow almost anywhere in nearly anything that will hold soil and water, making them ideal for shallow planters placed in a kitchen greenhouse window or hung from a deck railing within a few steps of the back door. For small-space gardens composed mainly of containers, herbs provide a wide range of choices.

Herbs, in fact, even have a pot designed for them—a rounded, vertical container featuring multiple openings that allow several varieties to thrive in the same vessel. Its shape and construction also afford you the ability to rotate the pot so the plants gain adequate sun exposure or, conversely, so that sensitive varieties can be shielded.

In pots, invasive herbs such as mint and rosemary can be prevented from spreading yet retain their aroma and yield enough for most needs. In addition to their culinary benefits, herbs also have an established reputation as promoters of good health and even medicinal relief. They provide a natural supplement or replacement for Western medicines used to treat cold and flu, muscle and joint pain, and stress, among other ailments.

Like vegetables, herbs benefit most from virgin potting soil mixed with a healthy dose of organic material and slow-release nutrients (about one-third the total soil volume), plus a fertilizer boost every two to three weeks, depending on how much water the plant has been receiving.

Plant herbs at the beginning of the gardening season—most are perennials, and the early spring growth will give them time to mature and permit harvest by midsummer. If they become too leggy, pinch or cut them back to promote new, bushy growth.

Set in a kitchen windowbox or deep sill, an herb garden provides the cook with easy access to fresh-grown herbs to spice any culinary creation.

PLANTING HERBS
IN CONTAINERS

With shallow roots and moderate growing cycles, most herbs can be planted in just about any type or size of container. To allow herbs to mature and yield without crowding each other, however, a squat container with ample surface area, like the one shown here, is perfect. Just follow these simple steps:

1 Fill the container with fresh potting soil—a standard mix of medium density is ideal for most herb plants.

2 Gently ease starts out of their nursery containers by inverting each container and tapping to release the plant. Take care to avoid disturbing their root systems. Position each plant to allow for growth.

3 Notch out a hole in the soil to the same dimensions as that of the nursery container, using it as a guide.

4 Compact the soil around each plant and create a slight mound around the stem.

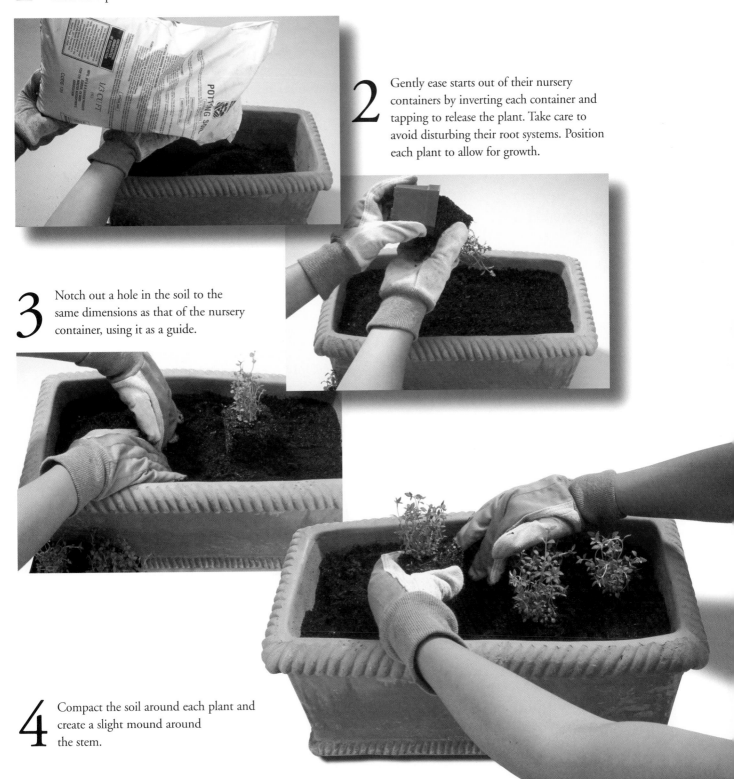

SHRUBS IN CONTAINERS

Shrubs in containers quite literally are what you make of them, which is to say that your choice of plants, where you choose to locate them, and how you shape them will determine their stature in your garden.

Compared to shrubs commonly used to border an open garden, the typical container shrub offers a few more options. Varieties that bloom, such as gypsophila, or those that produce berries, as do some evergreens such as holly or pyrecantha, can be moved to spotlight certain areas, then moved again to perform more of a supporting role—becoming a canvas of texture and solid color to highlight flowers grown in front of them. Similarly, deciduous varieties can be moved to an area that will showcase their fall colors, or placed alongside evergreen shrubs for striking contrast.

In addition, a row of small shrubs can be grouped together to define a border or other area of the garden, while taller varieties, such as bamboo, can create privacy or screen unsightly views.

More substantial than flowers but not quite as assuming as trees, shrubs require a slightly different planting scheme. Ideally, shrubs are best planted in the spring, though in mild climates they can be potted in autumn or even midwinter so they reach their peak in the spring and summer. Healthy shrubs should be transplanted from nursery pots to containers that are a few inches wider and deeper; subsequent repottings should be done biannually, allowing for a gradual increase in pot size to accommodate root growth.

To repot a shrub, use standard, lightweight potting soil with fertilizer. Once the new pot is nearly full of soil, press the old pot into the new one to form a planting hole for the rootball. Invert the original container, holding the shrub at the base of its stem, and tap gently to loosen the roots. Place the plant and firm the new soil around it.

Most shrubs respond well to sheltered locations that get a fair share of sun but little wind (varieties that grow quite tall, such as plumbago and bamboo, perform poorly in windy conditions). In mild climates, trim back shrubs after they bloom, severely trim shrubs that are overwintered, and protect them from frost; they will develop new, bushy growth the following season.

Topiary—the art of shaping growing plants—is easy. Shrubs are among the plants most amenable to creativity. Most can be trained and trimmed easily to meet a variety of needs in the garden.

Amid all the flower pots and windowboxes found in most container gardens, potted trees are sometimes overlooked. From Japanese maples to junipers, locust, and citrus, trees can be a container garden's anchor, providing maturity, scale, and permanence.

TREES IN CONTAINERS

Planting trees in containers is similar to the method used for other potted plants [see Planting Trees and Shrubs, pg. 63]. Though they can be planted at any time of year, autumn and spring are optimal. Before you buy, make sure that the tree is not rootbound. The pot you choose should be sized to the tree—that is, twice the width and depth of the existing root system. Another rule of thumb is to allow a foot (30 cm) in container diameter for every 4 feet (120 cm) of tree height.

Trees require no special soil mixes; some species, such as Japanese maple, need a little acidic additive, and the soil should include a slow-release organic fertilizer to kick-start the transplant. When planting, fill the container to the same level as its nursery pot. Keep the soil loose, tamping gently around the roots. Add a support stake or two, if necessary.

Watering is the primary concern for trees in containers. When dry, a tree stops growing; the restrictions of even a large vessel, when combined with a lack of nutrients and water, will dwarf or stunt any tree. When the tree begins to require daily watering, it's a sign that it needs a larger pot—about an additional 4 inches (10 cm) in diameter.

Pruning care is a small chore for container trees, amounting to snipping rogue stems and refining the tree's shape. Prune after bloom or in autumn.

The breadth and depth of a tree's rootball will help you determine the correct container size. Place the container in its ultimate location before planting unless you have the means to move it after planting. Filled containers, especially those weighted with water, are heavy and awkward to move.

Each spring, it's a good idea to remove the top 1–2 inches (25–50 mm) of soil and replace it with fresh mix; add a dose of fertilizer at the same time.

While many choices exist for container trees, the best candidates are dwarf and slow-growing varieties. Others, like pines and junipers, naturally are adapted to dry soil conditions, which is common in many containers. Conifers, especially evergreens, put up with root restriction better than most trees, requiring less food and nutrients than broad-leaf species.

A potted tree can anchor and focus your garden, providing the elegance and prominence of statuary to an open setting.

FRUIT TREES AND VINES IN CONTAINERS

Of all the plants suited to container gardening, fruit-bearing species are the most appealing yet the most difficult to maintain. Their payoff—fresh berries, figs, lemons, peaches, apples, and plums—makes the extra care well worth the effort.

As with all container gardening, planting a fruit tree or vine in a container has its advantages. It allows you to better protect the plant from frost or other climatic changes by moving it under cover or insulating it when necessary.

Most fruit-bearing plants are composed of two important parts: the rootstock (below the soil) and the scion (above the soil). The scion delivers the fruit, but the rootstock is the real key to the tree's or vine's vigor, in large part determining the size of the plant, its hardiness, and its ability to adapt to soil conditions.

For containers, nurseries and garden centers often offer hybrids—a dwarf-variety rootstock grafted to a scion bred to bear a full yield of fruit and grow full-sized branches and stems. Even better for containers are "genetic" dwarfs, in which both the scion and the rootstock are naturally smaller than those of other varieties.

Another key issue is pollination, which is essential to a fruit tree's or vine's ability to bear fruit. Some plants, such as the peach tree, self pollinate. Species that rely on cross-pollination, however, require the same or a closely related species blooming at the same time to sprout a crop. In container gardening, putting two plants in the same pot or adjacent to one another facilitates cross-pollination.

For deciduous tree species, select a sturdy container 2–3 inches (5–8 cm) wider than the roots of the plant. This pot, however, will serve only for one season, after which the tree should be transplanted to a more permanent home. For citrus, the recommended container diameter is 3–4 inches (8–10 cm) larger than the rootball; such varieties can be planted directly into their permanent containers.

Most good-quality potting soils are fine for many fruit trees and vines, though certain species like blueberries require a higher acidic content and peat moss in their mix. Deciduous varieties need a monthly dose of fertilizer throughout the spring and summer months.

As vital as pruning is to maintaining the size and shape of the scion, equally important is thinning the tree's yield by removing flowers and immature fruit before harvest. An abundant crop may sound like a nice problem to have, but too many fruits can reduce the average size of the fruit. In early spring, when most clusters begin to form from the blossoms, reduce each cluster to one fruit apiece, leaving about 6 inches (15 cm) between clusters.

Fruit-bearing plants often require more maintenance than other container plants. However, whether trees or vines, they add yet another level of texture, color, aroma, and taste to your garden.

PLANTING TREES AND SHRUBS

The right-sized container and the proper soil mixture are more critical to potted fruit trees than to other container plants. Root systems of fruit trees, berry- and grapevines must have enough room to grow if they are to satisfactorily grow and produce fruit. The plants must receive almost constant nourishment from fertilization every 3–4 weeks throughout the growing season. Choosing a mobile container will allow you to move a tree if there is a threat of frost—and to plant it where it is most convenient to you, according to the steps below:

1 After providing a drainage medium at the bottom of the pot, add the recommended soil and nutrients.

2 Once the soil and fertilizer are thoroughly mixed, create a hole deep enough for the plant's rootball and gently position the tree in the planting hole.

3 Gently compact the soil mix around the trunk, leaving the top of the rootball slightly exposed.

4 Water thoroughly and monitor for adequate drainage, both in soil absorption and in drainage from the bottom of the container.

FERNS IN CONTAINERS

With a history dating back 300 million years, their own age (the Carboniferous Period), and about 12,000 known varieties, ferns have a unique place in gardening lore. They offer a tremendous range of sizes and textures, visual interest, and focus, and are a unique backdrop to other flowers and plants.

One would think that these features would indicate ease of propagation, but growing ferns from scratch can be tricky. For this reason, transplanting ferns is the method of choice [see opposite].

Ferns love cool, moist environments. They can't tolerate heat or frost; such conditions will quickly kill even large specimens. Their foliage and fronds are delicate, especially when first forming, and benefit from misting throughout the first month or so of development. Ferns generally are resistant to fungal diseases that would fell other container plants treated to their preferred regimen of cool, continuously damp (but not soggy) soil.

Unlike other seedlings and starters, young ferns require a significant adjustment period to the open air. For two weeks or so following transplant, place them in a cool, sheltered location outdoors with adequate protection from strong sunlight and heat and monitor the reaction of the plants. If they start to wither or change color, cover them, move them to a warmer location, and allow them to recover. Once they have adjusted to their final location, they will make durable and enduring additions to the garden.

Ferns are available in nearly every shape, form, and texture. They grow in heights from those suited to low containers to those as tall as trees. Rely on expert advice to help tailor the planting to your site; garden store personnel in retail outlets that stock fern varieties are a good source of information.

Growing ferns from scratch can be tricky, but transplanting them into containers is simple. Ferns provide a dramatic backdrop to flowers, but their textures and subtle shadings frequently are interesting enough in themselves to attract favorable comment.

TRANSPLANTING A FERN

Ferns are easily grown from nursery transplants. Most varieties require less light than other annual and perennial plantings, allowing you to bring subtle color and texture to dark or stark corners of rooms or shady garden niches. Follow these easy steps:

1 In a standard mix of fresh potting soil with a slightly acidic pH, carve a space deep enough to accommodate the fern's root system, using the nursery container as a guide.

2 Position the fern so that it receives exposure to light on all sides, or plant it in a container that can be turned to assure even growth.

3 Water the fern immediately after planting and daily for the first 10 days. Thereafter, gradually reduce the frequency of watering until the plant receives water every 4–5 days. Soil should be kept moist, but avoid standing water.

ROSES IN CONTAINERS

When it comes to container gardening, a rose is still a rose—in other words, an ideal container plant. While certain roses, most notably miniatures, are more suited to containers than are others, many varieties share characteristics with their larger brethren, including scent, beauty, care, and pruning needs.

Even if you choose a compact rose, you'll need a pot large enough to support its root system—at minimum 18 inches (45 cm) in diameter for a single plant. Like all containers, the pot needs to drain freely; a moderately porous container is okay, but one that dries out too quickly can be fatal to roses, which thrive in direct sunlight during their peak growing and blooming season.

Many roses are sold in spring as bare roots, that is, free of any soil or container. Bare-root roses allow you to examine and evaluate the health of the entire plant before you make your purchase. A branching trio of strong, green, well-spaced root stems (or "canes") is ideal—soft, discolored, and tangled roots should send up a red flag.

Because roses rely on direct sun to bloom but can dry out easily in containers, shade their pots but make sure the plant gets sunlight. Best are spots such as a covered entry or just under porch eaves. Such a placement also helps ensure some shade for both plant and pot by midafternoon.

The royalty of any garden, roses add a sensuous element either alone or grouped together. Container roses need more frequent watering than roses grown in open ground. Always water them at the base of the plant to limit potential for mildew or other fungal disease.

Pruning is essential to achieving the bloom and growth you want from potted roses. The goal in pruning is to create an open and upward fan of branches, free from each other and any crossing stems. Most roses rely on new growth for their bloom, so such old growth is simply superfluous and likely will appear thorny and bare.

In the spring, as new buds start to form, cut out the dead, spindly, and crossing branches and leave three or four buds per remaining stem. An angled cut just above the last outward-facing growth will promote a bushy appearance and a better bloom.

Like its stems, a rose's roots can become tangled. After a few years in a container, remove the plant and prune it down to a few healthy, well-spaced roots, then replant it in fresh potting soil.

Miniature varieties of roses tend to thrive better in containers than do their full-sized counterparts. Though the flowers tend to be smaller, their clustered bloom patterns can be dramatic.

PLANTING BARE-ROOT ROSES

In contrast to most nursery starts, bare-root roses come without soil already protecting their roots. While this allows you to check for the health and firmness of the root system, it requires a special—though relatively easy—technique for planting, as shown below:

1 A bare-root rose requires a container that will support its root system adequately, such as the one shown here.

2 With a drainage medium at the bottom, fill the container with medium-density potting soil and mound it to the center.

3 Center the stem on the top of the mound, then gently spread the roots in a circular fan.

4 Still holding the stem, backfill the container with soil and compact it gently around the roots.

5 To add stability, insert a vertical support, taking care to place it outside the reach of the plant's roots. Loosely tie the plant to the stake using stretchy plastic plant tape.

Your plants are in their pots, on their way to delivering the flowers, foliage, or edible treats you envisioned when you started planning your garden. As veteran gardeners know, at this point you're only halfway home.

Like any garden, container gardens require nurturing to keep the plants healthy, productive, and attractive. The particular challenges of container gardening begin with the simple fact that a pot is an unnatural place for flowers and other plantings. Soil dries out faster in containers, roots can become cramped, and containers are prone to drainage and decay problems.

In addition, because potted plants usually have high visibility—they line the front steps, adorn a patio or deck, flank garden benches—poorly tended or neglected container gardens can be as painful to the eye as they are to the grower's ego.

On the plus side, many containers are mobile, allowing you to protect plants as the weather shifts, alter their exposure to sun and shade, and keep them conveniently close for proper care and maintenance. Also, because they are, well, contained, managing the care of container plantings is not overwhelming, nor does it require a great deal of time. If there should be a plant failure, replacement is a simple matter, too.

In this chapter, you'll learn all the easy steps to caring for a container garden—how to water and mist, fertilize and prune, control pests and diseases, use available light or add light, and include succession-planting methods for a year-round garden that is visually pleasing.

> The secret to caring for container plants is consistency— in watering, fertilizing, and pest control

Caring for Container Gardens

Correct watering— including the amount, frequency, and method—is the most essential care consideration of container gardens.

WATERING

More than just an essential nutrient or part of a larger maintenance regimen, water is a plant's lifeblood, with obvious results when it is provided or held back. In an open garden, plants can extend their roots to find moisture when the soil around them runs dry. In a container, however, that option is blocked by the container.

For this reason, and because soil in a pot dries out more easily, any plant in a container generally requires more (and more regular) watering than one planted in open ground. The general rule for almost all plant varieties, placed indoors or out, is to keep the soil moist but not soggy during the growing season. Often, the best moisture indicator is a finger plunged 2–3 inches (5–8 cm) into the soil. Visual observation is another effective method, as damp soil is often darker than dry soil. Wilting leaves or flowers also can indicate stress from lack of water, and a pot with a dry plant typically will weigh less than one properly saturated with water.

Once you have determined the watering needs of your container plant, consider the time of day to water. During the growing season, usually spring and summer, watering in the early- to midmorning hours allows the roots to absorb moisture with minimal loss from evaporation, giving them strength to weather the midday heat. On particularly hot or windy days, another splash at dusk will replenish a plant's roots. Because water also can be absorbed through foliage, a gentle misting up to midday will provide a boost.

In winter or dormant months, watering needs can shift dramatically to perhaps once a week or less. For outdoor container plants in cold climates, late morning is often the best time (if there's a threat of frost, hold off); when overnight frost is more likely, a winter evening's watering should always be avoided.

Plants in unglazed terra-cotta pots (above) generally require frequent watering. Misting (top right) helps plants absorb water through their foliage.

CONTAINER WATER NEEDS

Container gardens have a greater tendency to dry out, even with regular watering. If this occurs, try some of these simple solutions:
- Repot the plant in a larger and less-porous container, and mix a fresh batch of soil with some polymers—jellylike nodes that hold several times their size in water, thereby reducing the need for watering.
- Put the pot into a larger container and surround it with peat moss to help slow evaporation and other moisture loss from the smaller pot.
- Group pots together, allowing their plantings to shade each other and their containers.
- Pull out weeds and other dead, unproductive, or wayward growth, all of which saps moisture and nutrients from the plantings.
- Mulch the soil surface with bark or pebbles.
- Install a drip tray under the pot to capture drainage, which can then wick back up into the soil as the temperature rises; be sure to drain or suction the tray by dusk to avoid waterlogging.
- Be wary of drainage—conventional wisdom says that a plant is sufficiently watered when it begins to drain, but that's not always the case, especially if the water drains quickly; in such cases, submerge the pot above its rim in a bucket of water and when no more bubbles appear, it means the rootball has been adequately saturated.

Innovative accessories allow proper watering while protecting delicate foliage, reaching thirsty roots, and mitigating soil displacement.

When the food runs out, a container plant has nowhere to go to replenish the stock—it must depend on you. (Even potting mixes that contain nutrients have nothing left to give after a month or two: the nutrients are taken up by the roots or lost through drainage.) Most often the solution is simply to mix in some fertilizer twice a month with waterings, or periodically add compost as a topdressing.

For plants, the most common and necessary nutrient in a balanced "diet" is nitrogen. It helps leaf development and a plant's outward (visible) health and growth. Nitrogen deficiency shows itself most commonly by turning the leaves a pale shade of green or yellow; an abundance of this nutrient, on the other hand, can delay a plant's bloom or crop.

(Above) Diluting certain fertilizers in water allows faster absorption but also reduces their long-term efficacy.

The other primary plant nutrients are potassium, for hardiness and color, and phosphorus, for root formation. Potash can counteract an overdose of nitrogen; if leaves lack potassium, however, they may become scorched looking or discolored around their edges. As with nitrogen, an excess dosage of phosphates can stunt growth.

(Left) In granular form, whether mixed into the potting soil during planting or used as a topdressing during the growing season, fertilizers have a longer-term effect on the plant.

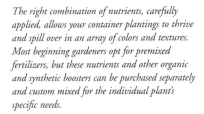

Nitrogen, potassium, and phosphorus are available in "complete" fertilizer form, separately, or in combinations of two, so gardeners can mix their own fertilizer to meet the particular needs of certain plants. Generally, foliage or leafy plants with limited blooms require more nitrogen, while flowering plants often need extra potassium and a lesser dash of nitrogen during their growth season.

Fertilizers are either organic (derived from plant or animal matter, such as manure) or inorganic (created from mineral sources). Because organic fertilizers are less soluble in water, they are slower acting and longer lasting, reducing the frequency of feeding chores. They're also bulkier.

When you apply fertilizer in any form, make sure the soil is moist by watering, that the day is cloudy or the temperature is cool, to mitigate the potential for chemical burn or leaf scorching.

The right combination of nutrients, carefully applied, allows your container plantings to thrive and spill over in an array of colors and textures. Most beginning gardeners opt for premixed fertilizers, but these nutrients and other organic and synthetic boosters can be purchased separately and custom mixed for the individual plant's specific needs.

APPLYING FERTILIZER

Fertilizers are available in solid, liquid, or water-soluble form, as organic or synthetic chemicals, in combination with potting soils or alone. For success, always follow the label's application instructions to the letter. Container plants benefit from applications of organic fertilizers in the form of well-rotted manure, compost, or fish-emulsion liquids. For midseason fertilizing, granular products are convenient and easy to apply. Follow these steps whenever you apply granular fertilizer:

1 Measure the correct amount of fertilizer granules, following the manufacturer's package label instructions for the particular type of plant.

2 Apply the fertilizer in a circular pattern around the perimeter of the pot where the plant's roots are located.

3 With a hand fork, mix the fertilizer into the surface of the soil until it has been completely incorporated.

4 Water the plant thoroughly until water begins to drain from the pot, then let it drain completely before replacing it in its location. Never leave plants in standing water.

PRUNING

Pruning can be an intimidating task. For some, it seems antithetical, even though proper shaping, trimming, and thinning keep plants going strong from season to season. Other gardeners regard it as something of an annoyance—like getting a haircut. But this opinion changes in a few months, when the pruned plant is full of bursting blooms and shiny foliage. Like that haircut, few things are irreversible in gardening; in fact, if a pruning "mistake" means cutting a stem or branch back a little further to properly direct a growth pattern, chances are it was for the best.

As a measure for maintaining a healthy plant, pruning includes the removal of dead or dying stems or branches—plus those that are weak, ill, or off course—so that the strongest and straightest can thrive. Occasionally, pruning also means clipping flowers, but usually toward the end of their bloom. Annuals, in particular, need to be cut back as soon as the seedhead starts to form on the dying bloom. Called deadheading, this pruning practice halts an annual's natural urge for propagation in favor of more flowers and a longer blooming season. To accomplish it, simply cut the seedhead back to the flower stem joint, or pinch off growth tips between your thumb and forefinger.

When to prune is determined by whether a plant relies on a previous year's growth or entirely new growth to produce flowers or other yield the next year. Hydrangeas and camellias, for example, bloom on old growth; azaleas and many roses require new growth to flower. Prune the former at the end of the season, in anticipation of the following year's growth; the latter, when buds appear or during a plant's dormant months. It's always the right season to thin out unproductive growth, remove diseased or dead foliage and flowers, cut to train a climber, or shear a shrub to refine or reduce its shape.

Deadheading—the procedure of clipping wilting blooms—allows new annual or perennial flowers to continue blossoming, effectively extending the season.

Not just a shaping method, pruning helps control root growth—especially important in the confines of a container—while also keeping your plants looking fresh and well tended. Cut all straggly or weak growth from the center of the plant to direct energy toward the stronger branches. Shape the plant by cutting right above latent buds.

Pinching is a hands-on method of removing old growth to encourage further blooms or bushier clusters. Take the foliage to be removed between your thumb and forefinger, and pinch it off.

CONTROLLING PESTS

Pests are an unfortunate aspect of any garden, containers included. Luckily, they're not difficult to control, especially if you practice good plant hygiene and know what makes plants susceptible to insects and other predators that feed on plants.

The key to pest control starts with the plants you select and, to a lesser extent, the soil mix and containers you use. Some plants are more susceptible to pests, especially non-native varieties introduced into an unfamiliar hardiness zone with its own set of pests and diseases [see Appendix, pg. 127]. Other plants have natural resistance that thwarts pests. Knowing when and why a plant is vulnerable to pests—and what type of pests they are—goes a long way toward preventing a larger problem.

With that knowledge, an ounce of prevention and proper plant hygiene can keep pests under control. For instance, soil mix intended for reuse should be sterilized. Better yet, purchase new soil; at the very least, avoid using the same soil for the same variety of plant, as latent pests (eggs or larvae) buried in the mix are likely to have acquired a taste for the plant. Always sterilize containers—whether new or recycled—to kill off any residue from bugs or fungi [see Sterilizing Containers, pg. 42].

Prevention also will mitigate the potential for bigger problems. Periodic inspections, including digging into the soil for burrowing bugs and turning over leaves, will allow you to catch the early stages of infestation. So, too, will diligent removal of dead, dying, or diseased material, and hand picking pests when you spot them.

A potential scourge of any garden, pests (such as the aphids shown here) can be controlled easily and most effectively through preventive care.

Other preventive measures include regular garden care, such as watering properly and maintaining optimum culture and shade conditions. A strong, healthy plant simply is better able to ward off attack than one weakened by neglect. Also, keep your garden clean and hardscape areas swept—debris is a perfect breeding ground for pests.

If an infestation does get out of hand and requires chemical control measures, remember: such remedies are hazardous. Follow package instructions to the letter, wear protective clothing and gloves, properly dispose of containers, and thoroughly clean any equipment used to apply the chemicals. Also, target the solution to the specific pest and apply it only to the affected area, never to the surroundings.

If you must resort to chemical means to rid your garden of pests, always wear hand and eye protection, spray on a completely windless day, and use a respirator. Apply pesticides only to infested areas.

APPLYING INSECTICIDAL SOAP

Ordinary soap and commercial preparations that contain mild insecticides are effective pest-control agents only when applied directly to the insect nuisance. They act by disrupting the pests' ability to breath. They are generally less toxic than either biological or synthetic chemical pesticides, are less harmful to the environment, and degrade quickly. Use them as shown whenever an outbreak is first noticed:

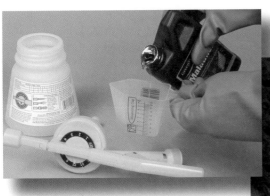

1 Following all package instructions and wearing protective gloves, mix the soap solution in a misting hand sprayer.

2 Apply the insecticidal soap directly to the insect pests, making sure to spray both the tops and bottoms of leaves as well as any infested stems.

USING HOSE-END SPRAYERS

1 When infestations are severe, use a hose-end sprayer to apply soaps or pesticides. Measure carefully to dilute the control agent, following the package and sprayer instructions completely. Always wear protective clothing and gloves when mixing and applying pest-control solutions.

2 Applicators mix hose water with the solution at either a fixed or a variable rate. Apply pesticides only on windless days.

3 Exercise care when disposing of empty pesticide containers. Wrap the container in newspaper, then dispose of it with the household trash or take it to a community hazardous-waste collection site.

CONTROLLING FUNGUS AND DISEASE

Fungal diseases and other infections can spread rapidly if left untreated. Fortunately, signs of them on container plantings are readily detectable. The best method of control is prevention—in the form of proper plant care and maintenance.

Unlike pests, fungal attacks and other plant disorders or ailments can be seen only by observing the symptoms, which include rusted leaves or black-spotted fruit. By the time symptoms are visible, enough damage already may have been done to warrant quarantine or removal of the plant.

In container gardening, such risks and hazards are less prevalent than in an open garden. Plant diseases are most likely to occur when conditions can't support the nutritional needs of a plant. Because you control the soil content, quality, and nutrients in a container garden, the natural infections and imperfections of open soil are greatly reduced. With virgin potting soil and a dose of fungal inhibitors, you can eliminate the vast majority of fungi and diseases that plague plants in an open garden.

The mobility of many containers allows you isolate plants that are ill, whether from disease or, more likely, a nutritional imbalance. By physically separating a diseased plant from its healthy neighbors, you can address the malady on a more controllable scale with a remedy that treats the specific plant without affecting others.

When you select a plant, research its susceptibility or resistance to certain diseases and find out how its diseases typically are spread—through the soil, by pests, or by pollination—and what can be done to prevent or discourage them.

Lastly, bone up on common plant diseases to find out how, what, and when they attack, as well as their symptoms and warning signs. Gray mold, for example, affects leaves, stems, flowers, fruit, and even bulbs. It's transmitted by insects or through injury; the infected tissue turns yellow and eventually rots to a furry mold, which can spread quickly through dustlike spores to neighboring plants.

The best solution to plant disease is, of course, prevention. A healthy plant will be less susceptible to disease, fungi, or mold and better able to resist and fight them off should they attack. Some experts call these preventive measures "good cultural practice"—that is, creating and maintaining garden conditions that, by design and care, discourage a scourge. Consider watering, for instance: dousing a plant from overhead may be easier, but chances are you're not only wasting water but also promoting mold and mildew. Also, proper drainage, specifically keeping drain holes clean and clear, lessens the chance of soggy soil—a breeding ground for diseases and fungi. In addition to isolating infected or ill plants, space your container plants far enough apart to let air circulate between them. Also, keep your garden tidy to reduce the development and spread of diseases harbored in debris and discarded organic matter.

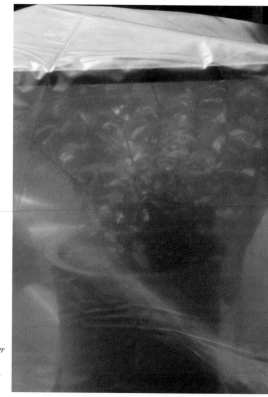

Isolation is an effective way to care for an ill plant while containing the problem. You also can protect healthy plants from infection by putting them under cover in much the same way. Allow space between foliage and the cover to prevent condensed moisture from contacting the plant.

APPLYING CHEMICAL PESTICIDES

Severe pest infestations sometimes resist environmentally preferable methods of control. More often, they occur when previous pesticide applications have reduced populations of beneficial insect predators. Chemical pesticides are either synthetic or natural plant compounds. They usually are hazardous to humans and always should be used with caution, following completely the manufacturer's recommendations and package-label instructions. Apply pesticides following these steps:

1 Identify the pest and select a pesticide that specifically lists that insect on its label. Always wear protective clothing, gloves, and a respirator.

3 Apply the solution on a windless, cool day, only to the infested area. Do not apply it to unaffected areas, and avoid contact with spray mist. Always wash thoroughly with soap immediately after applying pesticides.

4 Remember: store and discard all pesticides safely. Avoid pouring out unused concentrate; allow it to evaporate outdoors instead. Wrap empty bottles in newsprint for safe disposal.

PREVENTING CONTAINER PROBLEMS

For all of its advantages, gardening in containers also has its trials. Ask any seasoned container gardener to pinpoint them and you'll get a laundry list of failures.

It bears repeating: a pot is not a natural habitat for a plant. This makes the reasons for failure less obvious than for plants grown in open ground.

The key to all gardening is to head off problems before they happen. If there is a single formula for success with container gardening, it is this: buy healthy plants, put them in clean pots of an appropriate size for the eventual growth of your plantings, use the right soil and nutrients, and water and fertilize them as needed.

The improper match of plant to pot is likely the reason behind the symptoms of a struggling specimen. Choose the wrong-sized container or one made of an unsuitable material, or neglect proper preparation, and you soon will have a container with only wilted plants and a mound of soil. The next most common reason for failure of container plants is improper watering—too little or too much.

On the other hand, if you choose wisely, prepare properly, and keep in mind that container gardens generally need more water than open gardens, you may be able to nurture species you never thought were possible to grow in your area's climate and conditions.

The type and size of container—and particularly its ability to retain water and moisture—is important in determining a plant's watering needs. Both underwatering (top) and overwatering (above) are equally detrimental.

(Top right) Yellowed foliage usually indicates a fertilizer deficiency or an acid-balance problem that can be corrected through feeding.

In the proper container, a plant is allowed to thrive; even a sick or dying plant can be revived if given the correct treatment.

ADJUSTING FOR CHANGING LIGHT

As temperature and climate conditions change with the progression of the seasons, so does the amount and intensity of light shed on your container garden. Exposure also is affected by the growth of surrounding trees and of other container plantings and by shading from structures as the position of the sun changes.

Though plants differ in their requirements for light, all need it to some degree to perform photosynthesis, the natural manufacture of food in the form of carbohydrates, which provides nourishment for growth and good health.

In general, a plant's foliage indicates its light needs: the greener the leaves, the less light the plant requires. Plants with colored or variegated foliage, by contrast, need more light. In both cases, a lack of sufficient light will cause colors to fade and foliage either to droop or to drop from the plant.

Plants that rely on a great deal of sunlight must be monitored for signs of heat exhaustion or scorching. While direct sunlight may be essential for such plants, intense heat can sear tissues and dry out soil and roots. A few hours in partial shade during a particularly hot day likely will benefit a plant more than enough to offset the reduced photosynthesis during that time.

A container garden may enjoy full sun during part of the day, but in the morning or afternoon, trees and structures may cast shadows. Consider these changes when choosing your plantings.

As winter approaches and you prepare to move your plants indoors for protection [see Protecting Plants from Cold, pg. 81], give them adequate time to adjust. A light-loving plant that enjoys being surrounded by sun all day may be ill suited to a corner location, even with a good window exposure. Supplement the light source with a full-spectrum fluorescent lamp and regularly rotate the plant so it achieves full light exposure. Also, when you move plants in and out of the house, ease the transition by moving them first to partial-shade areas.

There is a wide gallery of plants that tolerate or even prefer full or open shade. Under extremely hot conditions, even sun lovers can benefit from being placed in shade during the heat of the day.

ADJUSTING FOR SEASONAL CHANGE

A heavy dose of water at mid-morning is a must—even for sun-loving plants—during the peak of summer. It helps them withstand the heat of day.

As seasons change, so do the needs of container gardens. Though all gardens require some care year-round, if there's a true start to a container gardener's year, it's the spring. In a real sense, that's when things begin to happen, container-wise.

In cold-winter climates, plants taken indoors before the last frost are returned outdoors, and in all climates new seedlings and cuttings are potted and set in place. Trees are topdressed and trimmed for new growth, and foliage is washed, allowing the plant to drink in fully the burgeoning spring and early-summer sun.

As summer approaches and the sun's rays become harsher, your plantings will require additional watering and a watchful eye for scorched leaves and hungry pests. Also, as cool-season annuals begin to die back, you'll want to replace them with warm-season varieties.

With the coming of autumn, sun-loving plants that will be moved indoors can be eased into their new environment by first placing them in filtered-shade locations outdoors. Each plant that will be brought inside for the winter should be repotted into a smaller container, then returned to its original container in the spring. Doing so helps the plant become dormant.

If you don't have enough indoor space to accommodate all of your container plants, consider cutting new or recent growth from your perennials, then potting and overwintering them. Most contained trees and shrubs simply can be moved under roof eaves and covered with an insulating sheet in mild-winter climates.

Winter is a time of relative ease. Any plants that you've brought indoors actually need rest, so do not fertilize any but autumn or winter cuttings, and water them minimally; keep bulbs and tubers in a dry, room-temperature environment; and rotate dormant sun-loving plants from a southern to a western window exposure as the sun moves.

If you are bereft for tasks, this is the time to repair or upgrade your containers, watering systems, and tools. Before you know it, the last frost will have passed and the planting cycle will begin again.

Protecting late-blooming annuals and perennials from frost by covering them (below) or moving them to protected areas (right) will allow you to prolong enjoyment of their blooms during the day.

PROTECTING PLANTS FROM COLD

The onset of autumn means that it is time to move tender perennials and shrubs to cool, indoor locations in cold-winter climates or under shelter in milder areas. Protection from frost can take place in a heated greenhouse, or you can protect individual plants following the steps shown here:

2 Drill corner holes into the support frame, using a ½-in. (12-mm) power-drill bit. Cut four pieces of ½-in. (12-mm) dowel to a length sufficient to extend 4 in. (10 cm) above the tallest of the foliage. Insert the dowels into the corner holes, creating a support for plastic film.

1 Using care to avoid lifting strain, place the container onto a roller support that easily can be moved between garden and storage.

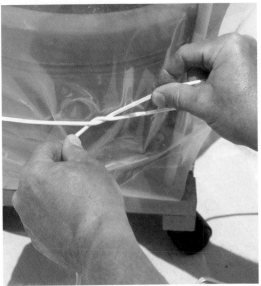

3 Drape sheet plastic film (available from hardware and home stores) over the dowel frame, securing it with waterproof tape to form a mini-greenhouse. Cut holes to let air circulate to the plant. The plastic should not touch the plant foliage at any point.

4 Secure the plastic film by loosely tying cord around the container. Remember that the cover must be lifted for periodic watering.

For many, the pleasure of gardening is in the process: digging your hands into soil, feeling the texture of a young leaf, smelling a ripening vegetable. Rarely is there a point at which any garden is "complete"—in fact, half the satisfaction of a garden is that it is an ever-changing canvas.

> Container gardens are perfect to share with neighbors, friends, and family

Decorating with container plants is an easy and highly noticeable way to express your personal style, regardless of your tastes or skill level. With both plants and pots from which to choose—not to mention the many locations available indoors and out—the possibilities are endless. You can take container planting a step further by adding your own decorative touches to a container or by mixing different types of plants in unique combinations of colors and textures.

In this chapter, you'll get some tips about decorating with containers, beginning with ideas for arranging your potted garden to enhance a variety of settings. Because color has a significant impact on any garden, there's also some insight into combining and contrasting warm and cool colors and using the palette to create the perception of depth.

Decorating with Containers

Similar to color, the texture of your plants adds dimension. It also creates varying and interesting shadows and patterns throughout the day and can soften, refine, or frame an edge or a boundary. You'll learn how the form and shape of your plants and their containers can be blended or contrasted to help present an attractive garden that defines your personal style.

Finally, because unusual or whimsical containers are part of a highly personalized garden, you'll discover ways to modify a favorite article or antique to make it a suitable container for a range of plantings.

A pair of potted trees stands guard at the front entrance to a home, complementing the formality and symmetry of the architecture while adding life and color to the scene.

ARRANGING CONTAINERS

A cluster of containers affords many advantages: watering and maintenance chores are a snap; the combinations of colors, textures, and shapes are practically limitless; and you can swap out plantings at will to freshen the arrangement.

Your container garden, like any garden, is an expression of your personal taste and style, but what do you do if it turns out looking more like the beast than the beauty? Most all of us can sense when something is out of proportion or misplaced; the problem is, we're not always sure how to fix it.

One great benefit of container gardening is that you can tinker with your arrangements more easily than you can with plantings in an open garden. Because container soils generally are of consistent quality, transplanting an ill-fitting specimen into another container will not cause it much trauma.

From a design standpoint, containers look best grouped in threes, with one large container anchoring two smaller ones in a triangular pattern. This trio arrangement can include containers of different shapes and materials [see Selecting Unusual Containers, pg. 88], but be aware that this will make a statement that's more about the containers than the plantings. On the other hand, grouping containers made from similar materials, such as terra cotta or wood, will focus more attention on your plantings. You can add interest by choosing containers cut from the same cloth, so to speak, but of different styles, colors, or textures.

A happy medium—and one that will attract attention to both pots and plantings—is to employ similar arrangements in different types of planters. This also works for a symmetrical arrangement (such as a pair of box planters, or cone-shaped pots or urns flanking a long, low-slung planter). Such formality is best suited to architecture of a similar symmetry, thereby providing a complement to it.

If your goal combines aesthetics with practicality, such as lining a path or walkway to lead folks to a garden scene or party location, use identical containers. Your imagination can then run wild with plantings. Create an arrangement with short plants graduating to tall, use flowers that present a spectrum of color, or simply establish a glorious expanse of your all-time favorites.

GROUPING AND ARRANGING CONTAINERS

Creating a pleasing visual arrangement using containers is the goal of every container gardener. One good starting point is to choose compatible planters with similar color tones. Here, earth tones unify the group. Tall and short plant forms also are helpful to define the arrangement. With these basics in mind, follow the steps shown:

1 Arrange the planters in an area. Note where plants run together or stand distinct from their neighbors.

2 Build a background tier comprising the tallest plants. Swap containers until the row is pleasing and full.

3 Using medium-height plants, construct a second row using their foliage to mask the containers behind.

4 Flank the sides of the arrangement with still smaller plants, each with distinctive blooms or foliage.

5 The completed group arrangement flows in a swath of color from the low plants at the front and sides to the tallest members in the rear, unifying the entire display.

BLENDING COLORS

The skillful use of color in a container garden commands respect as it draws attention and comment.

Staying within the basic color families—hot (red, yellow, and orange) or cool (blue, violet, and green)—when choosing flowers and foliage is a simple, safe, and attractive approach, creating visual harmony throughout a garden. Combining the two families can be effective in small spaces, as a singular burst to add focus to a garden. Combining brights with pastels is another step up but generally works only when flower or plant shapes and forms are similar.

To develop your color sense, start with something simple, like a collection of flowers or foliage in your favorite color. This is a time-honored approach, and you won't be disappointed when you behold a sea of red, blue, or yellow bursting forth from your garden. If you are happy with the result, try combining hues of the same color, such as lavender with plum purple or jade with kelly green.

From there, start moving around the color wheel, keeping in mind as you experiment that it's easy to get a little carried away. For relief, combine plantings that have broad, deep foliage with airier plants in neutral tones.

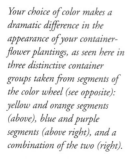

Your choice of color makes a dramatic difference in the appearance of your container-flower plantings, as seen here in three distinctive container groups taken from segments of the color wheel (see opposite): yellow and orange segments (above), blue and purple segments (above right), and a combination of the two (right).

USING A COLOR WHEEL

Color wheels, readily available at hobby and art stores, are used by artists and designers to visualize the colors they will use for paintings and other projects. Flower gardeners also can benefit by planning with color in mind. The wheel presents the primary colors—red, yellow, and blue—interspersed with their complements—orange, green, and violet. It also may be divided into "cool" and "warm" palettes. Follow the easy steps shown to create a pleasing color combination in a terra-cotta planter filled with brightly colored annual flowers:

1 Consult the color wheel as you choose flowers at the garden store. Here, primary red and yellow contrast with violet-blue to create drama and depth.

2 Arrange the plants, still in their store containers, within the planter until you achieve a pleasing arrangement. Then plant them in potting soil.

3 This planter features tall red snapdragons surrounded by yellow pansies, which contrast distinctly with the violet pansies.

SELECTING UNUSUAL CONTAINERS

While unusual and non-traditional containers can lend distinct style to your garden, they also must support the health and growth of the plantings they'll hold.

Any container, from a terra-cotta pot to a recycled wheelbarrow or work boot, must meet two basic criteria— hold enough soil for the plant selected and drain water properly. Be respectful of these requirements and, with proper preparation, success practically is assured.

The vessel also should be durable: if you must transfer a plant from a broken or rotted container before the plant takes root, it will suffer trauma. Some container choices are naturally tough, such as concrete chimney pots and troughs, old sink basins, and holders made of clay or galvanized metal. By contrast, old untreated wood or similar organic material filled with soil and set on the ground will break down eventually.

This "tricycle" (above) is only one example of the numerous whimsical "containers" currently available. An open windowbox (right) has a distinctive appearance; as the plants grow and spill over the edge, they will hide the container and appear to be growing out from the window.

If an unusual container is not suitable for planting, it still can be useful in the garden—as a sculptural piece, highlighting a pathway, or adding texture and color to a potted floral arrangement. Depending on its size and dimensions, it may be able to hold another, less interesting but better-suited pot. Old wood troughs, for instance, can define a border while housing several smaller containers filled with plants whose flowers will hide the planting pots.

As expressions of style and whimsy, unusual containers have their place in any garden setting. Keep in mind, however, that too much of an odd thing can get tiring to behold and can detract from the beauty and splendor of the plants. For maximum impact, place just one or two container treasures in highly visible locations.

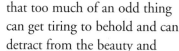

Given proper drainage and space for a plant's root growth, almost anything—including an old soda-pop crate—can serve as an adequate container. Used sparingly, novelty vessels can add character and charm to your garden.

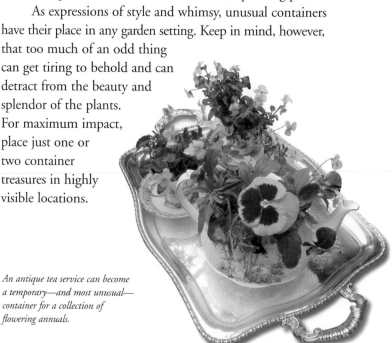

An antique tea service can become a temporary—and most unusual— container for a collection of flowering annuals.

PREPARING UNUSUAL CONTAINERS

Antique shops and garage sales are great places to unearth container treasures. Depending on their heritage, however, they may require modification to support healthy plants. Remember that attractive outer containers may house more suitable inner pots. Choose containers that are sturdy, and add drainage for your plants following these easy steps:

1 Many a stunning container begins its career in an antique store or flea market. Inspect each carefully and reject those with structural defects or finishes that will be ruined by soil or water.

2 Most non-planter containers lack suitable drain holes. To add them, first mark the center of the container's bottom and cover it with an X of masking tape to protect the container surface.

3 Using a ⅛-in. (3-mm) masonry drill bit set at low speed, drill a pilot hole through the container.

4 Mount a ⅝-in. (15-mm) drill bit and drill the drain hole, again using a slow motor speed.

5 Remove the masking tape, then rasp any burrs with a circular file. The container is now ready to receive a plant.

6 When watering, do so in a sink. Allow the plant to drain before returning it to the display area.

MATCHING AND CONTRASTING TEXTURES

Container gardens often are kept close at hand, allowing you to enjoy more intimately not only your plantings' colors, fragrances, or fruits, but also the textures and shapes of their foliage. Discovering at close range the shape and size of the leaves, and how a plant develops them, is one of the greatest delights of container gardening.

Foliage is categorized as having fine or coarse texture—that is, either small, delicate, or fine leaves and flowers; or large, long, and bold growth. As a general rule, fine-textured plants are best brought to the fore so that their structure can be appreciated, while large and coarse-leaved plants work best as backdrops, their lines and dimensions offering visibility from a distance and their deep colors delivering even coverage.

On the other hand, placing a broad- or coarse-leaved plant in front of taller, fine-textured foliage will give the illusion of depth; the opposite arrangement, such as a bed of wild grasses fronting a broad-frond fern, will make your garden seem shallower.

The relative gloss of a leaf also works into its texture. Matte or dull leaves tend to recede visually, while glossier foliage reflects light, highlighting the plant and its blooms or yield.

Understanding textures allows you to achieve the impact you want. Contrasting various textures, such as framing a fine-textured Japanese maple with an ornamental rhubarb or leopard plant, will draw attention to the tree. Blend similar textures, and the focus will be lost or concentrated only on the flowers or fruit.

If you're arranging smaller, individually potted plants, create an attractive blend by making subtle transitions from the finest foliage (such as a threadleaf cypress) to the broader varieties, such as hosta or lamb's ear, with medium-textured plants in between. Arranging your containers at different heights will expose as much of the foliage as possible.

(Above and top right) An arrangement of varying textures, including the relative gloss of each plant's foliage, can create the illusion of different depths.

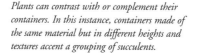
Plants can contrast with or complement their containers. In this instance, containers made of the same material but in different heights and textures accent a grouping of succulents.

MATCHING AND CONTRASTING FORMS

As with color and texture, blending plant forms and proportions is an integral component of a successful and attractive garden design. Properly mixing and contrasting plant forms provides dimension and draws attention to each plant, allowing it to be seen.

However varied your plantings or whatever the shape of your containers, the final result should be a pleasing geometric shape. When deciding on your plants and containers, consider whether you want trees or shrubs in round pots, which will lend a domed or oval effect; trailers in hanging planters, which will create a conical profile; or upright plants in a square or rectangular vessel, which will impart a more formal look. The best plant arrangements, whether in a single pot or as a grouping of multiple containers, rely on a base of plantings of similar form. This provides a canvas for filling in with plants of contrasting form for visual relief and interest.

Proportion, or the size and scale of your plantings in relation to other plants and their containers, involves nothing more than planting tall plants in large containers and low-lying plants in smaller containers, then placing the planters in areas where they will neither overwhelm nor get lost in their surroundings. It's also possible to achieve some dramatic effects with contrasting combinations of plants and containers, such as topping a tall concrete urn with a low-lying trailer—but this technique requires a good design eye and should be used sparingly.

Finally, consider the architectural elements of the locations in which they will be placed as you choose both your plants and their container homes.

Before potting in any container, remember to anticipate a plant's growth habits and its shape and size at maturity. If you decide on slow-growing varieties, you may want to start them out in small pots, then transplant them to larger vessels as they grow. Also keep in mind the container's proposed location. If its eventual home is against a wall or another structure, place taller plants at the back; if the planter will be viewed from all sides, set the taller plants in the center and work outward.

Spikes, trailers, cones, and spreaders all work together to present a miniature garden in the confines of a single container. Be careful, though, to combine plants that have similar watering and maintenance needs, as was done in this cactus and succulent pot.

HARVESTING VEGETABLES

The great thing about vegetables is that they provide a beautiful and ever-changing landscape even when they're weeks away from picking. There's great pleasure in watching tomatoes and peppers as they turn color, and beans growing long and strong. There's even interest in watching onions and garlic, which begin to lose their foliage, and carrots and potatoes, whose greens begin to droop as they near harvest.

Harvesting vegetables from containers is virtually identical to harvesting them from an open garden. The advantage of container-grown vegetables is that usually they yield just the right amount of produce needed, ensuring maximum freshness and taste and alleviating most storage or preservation concerns.

The ripeness of most edibles can be determined not only by sight but also by a gentle touch. If you've ever cradled a ripe tomato in your hand after giving it the slightest twist or tug, you know the feeling; similarly, the firmness of a lettuce leaf tells you that it's ready to clip from the head and put onto a plate.

(Top) Those accustomed to the bland and starchy taste of grocery potatoes have a pleasant surprise in store with their first taste of home-grown varieties. Freshly dug container potatoes are rich in flavor and sweet with natural sugars.

Smell and taste also are valuable tools during harvest. Ripe onions provide a distinct odor and taste to indicate their readiness, as do melons and certain peppers. An herb's aroma also is an indicator of readiness, but avoid clipping more than a third of the foliage at any given time so that the plant can produce new shoots and restore its energy. Better yet, maintain a constant, small harvesting of herbs, thereby avoiding a disruption of the growth cycle.

Lettuce leaves should be harvested in a quantity that can be used soon after picking. After washing, dry the leaves in a spinner or with paper towels, bag them in plastic, and store in the vegetable compartment of the refrigerator. Do the same with peppers, cucumbers, beans, and root vegetables such as carrots and barrel-grown potatoes.

Dwarf varieties of your favorite vegetables—including the most popular container vegetable, tomatoes—come in an ever-expanding array. Many dwarf varieties have a higher success rate than vegetables grown in an open garden.

All gardeners know how special relationships with their plants can become. With container gardening, that rapport often is even more intimate. The simple act of potting a plant and watching it grow on a patio or window sill is a wondrous experience and a daily reminder of nature's beauty.

THE INTIMACY OF CONTAINER GARDENING

By design, container plants require more care and attention than bedded plants. They dry out faster, can outgrow their vessels, are more vulnerable to stress and neglect, and may need to be moved or separated for special care and convalescence when they get sick.

The benefits of container plants, however, far outweigh any burden. The mere proximity of most container gardens brings plants and flowers closer to our lives, delivering color and vibrancy to brighten areas. We can enjoy their flowers and fragrances, find solace in their foliage, eat the bounty of their produce and fruits, and discover the lives of butterflies and birds in their branches and blooms.

Many container gardens are closer at hand than open gardens, and their proximity and care needs often inspire more passion and further knowledge about gardening.

Container plants also offer the opportunity to experiment with unusual and non-native plants, and to learn about those found naturally outside a particular plant hardiness zone [see Appendix, pg. 131]. As such, container plants can force us out of our comfort zone and broaden our perspective and experience.

Potted plants also are ideal for sharing [see Growing Gifts, pg. 95]. Few gifts rival a live plant. They allow us to pass along a love for gardening and nature to others in a lasting way, perhaps fostering another, new relationship in the process.

The simple act of watching a plant grow on a window sill is a wondrous experience, often inspiring a special relationship.

CONTAINER GARDENING WITH CHILDREN

It's no wonder that containers are among the best ways to introduce gardening to children. Starting children off by gardening on a small and simple scale builds their confidence and interest. With potted plants, the experience is up close and personal and provides lessons in responsibility and attentive care.

Unlike requests to "help me weed" or commands to "mow the lawn," container gardening gives youngsters the whole picture, not just a chore. Most children aged four and up can start from the beginning and nurture a plant to maturity or beyond, gaining a lifelong fascination with gardening and developing a interest to share with you.

Indeed, there's no age limit to gardening. Preschoolers can plant grass seeds in hollowed-out eggshells or sunflowers in small paper cups, then watch, fascinated, as their plantings sprout on the window sill. Older kids can help transfer plants to larger pots—allowing them the experience of getting their hands dirty on purpose. Preteens can cultivate their own blend of colorful flowers or take a turn at vegetable gardening—where a single pot will keep the project close at hand. Teens can include their own projects in your larger garden scheme, giving them a real sense of participation and involvement.

A trip to the nursery or garden center is a great place to start. Offering everything from soil mixes to containers, tools, fertilizers, pest remedies, and, of course, the plants themselves, it's as good as a trip to the proverbial candy store.

Gardening teaches responsibility and other important lessons to children, while providing them with spectacular rewards.

Once you get your purchases home, however, remember the patience that gardening requires. For young children, keep maintenance chores to a minimum. Create a makeshift calendar or schedule of tasks to keep them engaged. Whatever you do, reserve their garden projects for them alone: if a plant should die from neglect, it can help teach them responsibility—or it may indicate merely that gardening was a passing interest.

Finally, make their projects simple yet challenging. Choose unusual plants that are native to your area, that are resistant to pests and diseases, and that require little special care. If gardening is an interest you can share, the chances of success will promote the activity, and the bloom will be on the rose.

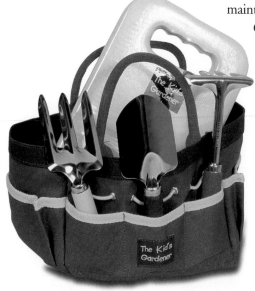

GROWING GIFTS

ew gifts rival the intimacy of a live plant. A potted azalea or a collection of different varietals in a hanging basket can brighten any space—and a container gift even can encourage a sick friend to recover and tend the plant. Just about any occasion, from a holiday to simply a celebration of the season, is appropriate for a growing gift. Best of all, a container plant is a lasting gift, whether it's an enhancement to an existing garden or a starter for a new one.

Perhaps the most special container gift is one culled from your own garden, with cuttings, starters, and even some seeds set in a specially chosen planter. If you're combining plants, make sure to select one dominant specimen and surround it with a pleasing combination of colors, textures, and shapes. The best combinations are those within the same hues or a blend of two complementary colors.

Dwarf trees or tall, blooming perennials often serve best as a focal point, delivering a vertical element as well as a basic background color and texture for seasonal flowers and trailers. Place your dominant plant in the center or, if it's likely the container will not be viewed from all sides, near the back of the planter.

Also consider the needs of your selections. Choosing plants with similar soil, watering, and fertilization requirements—and even growth habits—can make maintenance tasks infinitely simpler. Even though most plants likely will be native to your hardiness zone, depending on their species they may have differing care requirements. Finally, make sure your chosen container is large enough to handle the root systems and ultimate proportions of your selections.

Include a homemade list of instructions and helpful hints to keep the plantings healthy and thriving, especially as they mature and may need transplanting or pruning. A book about container gardening adds a nice finishing touch to the gift package.

The gift of a living plant is appropriate for any occasion, providing a lasting memory and perhaps inspiring or building on another container garden in the recipient's home.

Container gardening allows you to share a piece of your own garden with others or grow plants specifically intended for a friend or a family member.

*A*s with any type of gardening project, your primary focus is probably the plants. With container gardening, especially, your options are quite broad. In contrast to an open-garden project, your plant choices are less dependent upon soil conditions and climate. In containers, you can try non-native varieties and those from beyond your hardiness zone; employ indoor, overwintering, and other climate protection schemes; and provide particular environments with special potting soil mixes.

In addition, new plants specially engineered for containers, such as dwarf, miniature, and grafted varieties or hybrids of your favorite plants, make container plantings easier to manage. These varieties frequently produce a greater yield than their full-sized brethren, all in the context of a container.

The following encyclopedia of suitable container plants puts this wide world of plantings at your fingertips and all in one place so you can begin to fulfill your container gardening dreams. For the easiest reference, each plant is listed by its most common or recognizable name. (Professional horticulturists and botanists can refer to the cross-referenced index that lists both common and scientific plant names [see pg. 134].)

Every listing in this encyclopedia contains the most essential and useful information about each plant listed—including a full-color, close-up photograph that shows the details of each variety's foliage and, if appropriate, bloom or yield. In addition, you'll find facts about each plant: hardiness, classification, soil and nutrient requirements, care tips.

Container gardening, whether an exclusive venture or part of a larger, open-garden project, allows you to express your tastes and personality in a very intimate way. This gallery is meant to serve as your guide and starting point.

> **Nearly 100 plant varieties at your fingertips, with all the necessary visual and factual information to create great container gardens**

Encyclopedia of Container Plants

Container gardens come in all shapes and sizes, accommodating a staggering array of plants—in fact, there is hardly a plant that is not suited to some kind of pot. Best of all, container gardens, properly prepared for the site, can adorn almost any area of your home or landscape.

ANNUALS

Common name: Alyssum, Sweet
Scientific name: *Lobularia maritima*
Plant hardiness: Zones 2–10.
Foliage and bloom colors: Blossoms of white, lilac, pink, or purple. Leaves are narrow and green.
Soil needs: Moist, well-drained soil. Fertility: average. Overfeeding will lead to an abundance of foliage at the expense of flowers. Neutral 7.0 pH.
Light needs: Full sun.
Water requirement: Water regularly.
Spacing of plants: 6 in. (15 cm) apart.
Tips and care: Nice in a pot of mixed annuals. Cut back foliage if plant seems to be wilting in midsummer. When conditions cool it will come back with more blooms. Deadhead to promote further flowering. Attracts bees.

Common name: Asparagus Fern
Scientific name: *Asparagus densiflorus*
Plant hardiness: Zones 9–11.
Foliage and bloom colors: White star-shaped flowers. Fernlike branchlets with thin, needlelike leaves in bright to dark green.
Soil needs: Moist, well-drained soil. Fertility: average to moderately rich. Acid to neutral 6.5–7.0 pH.
Light needs: Full or partial sun.
Water requirement: Water moderately; try to keep soil just a bit moist.
Spacing of plants: 12–24 in. (30–60 cm) apart.
Tips and care: Flowers are fragrant. Combines well with almost any other plant. Can grow to 2 ft. (60 cm) tall, so allow for growth when choosing a container. Watch out for spider mites.

Common name: Baby Blue Eyes
Scientific name: *Nemophila*
Plant hardiness: Zones 2–10.
Foliage and bloom colors: Dainty bright-blue flowers with pale centers. Pale-green fernlike foliage.
Soil needs: Moist, well-drained soil. Fertility: moderately rich. Enrich with humus. Acid to neutral 6.5–7.0 pH.
Light needs: Full sun to partial shade.
Water requirement: Water moderately under average conditions; increase watering when weather is dry.
Spacing of plants: 6–12 in. (15–30 cm) apart.
Tips and care: A good trailing plant for a container or hanging basket. Does well in mountain climates.

Common name: Begonia, Wax

Scientific name: *Begonia* X *semperflorens-cultorum*

Plant hardiness: Zones 2–10.

Foliage and bloom colors: White, pink, or red flowers nearly cover the small mound of green foliage.

Soil needs: Well-drained, loamy soil. Fertility: rich. Supplement with peat moss, compost, or leaf mold. Neutral 7.0 pH.

Light needs: Partial sun.

Water requirement: Water frequently.

Spacing of plants: 8–10 in. (20–25 cm) apart.

Tips and care: Watch out for whiteflies, mealybugs, and leaf spot. Great for windowboxes and hanging baskets. Tolerates shade. Not very cold hardy.

Common name: Blue Star Creeper

Scientific name: *Laurentia axillaris*

Plant hardiness: Zones 5–10.

Foliage and bloom colors: Flowers are star-shaped, five-petaled, and light blue, lavender, or white arising from mounded foliage consisting of fine-textured, needlelike green leaves.

Soil needs: Moist, light, well-drained soil. Fertility: average. Acid 6.5 pH.

Light needs: Full sun.

Water requirement: Water moderately.

Spacing of plants: 4–6 in. (10–15 cm) apart.

Tips and care: This little-known but very attractive annual does well in hot weather in locations that are dry or have high humidity. Well suited to hanging baskets. Excellent when used as a groundcover used along walkways and borders.

Common name: China Pink Hybrids

Scientific name: *Dianthus chinensis*

Plant hardiness: Zones 5–10.

Foliage and bloom colors: Single or double flowers in red, pink, white, or bicolored. Slender green leaves.

Soil needs: Well-drained soil with a little lime mixed in. Fertility: rich. Use a diluted liquid fertilizer to avoid tip burn. Neutral to alkaline 7.0–7.5 pH.

Light needs: Full sun.

Water requirement: Water sparingly unless weather is very dry.

Spacing of plants: 6–12 in. (15–30 cm) apart.

Tips and care: Nice as a mass planting in a container. Flowers for months.

Common name: Chrysanthemum
Scientific name: *Chrysanthemum multicaule*
Plant hardiness: Zones 3–11.
Foliage and bloom colors: This variety sports bright-yellow daisylike flowers. Foliage is fleshy, smooth, narrow leafed, and green.
Soil needs: Moist, well-drained, loamy soil. Fertility: moderately rich to rich. Feed lightly but frequently. Neutral 7.0 pH.
Light needs: Full sun.
Water requirement: Keep soil moist.
Spacing of plants: 6–8 in. (15–20 cm) apart.
Tips and care: Attractive mixed in with other annuals such as snapdragon, larkspur, and lobelia. Watch out for aphids and spider mites. Favors cool weather.

Common name: Coleus
Scientific name: *Coleus blumei*
Plant hardiness: Zones 3–11.
Foliage and bloom colors: Foliage colors are the standout feature of this annual. Leaf colors are chartreuse, yellow, cream, pink, salmon, orange, red, green, or tricolored. Small blue flowers are fairly insignificant.
Soil needs: Moist, loamy, well-drained soil. Fertility: rich. Feed regularly with nitrogen liquid fertilizer. Neutral to alkaline 7.0–7.5 pH.
Light needs: Partial sun.
Water requirement: Water regularly.
Spacing of plants: Usually 10 in. (25 cm) apart, but can crowd in a pot.
Tips and care: Excellent foliage plant to highlight accompanying flowers that share coleus-leaf color. Watch out for slugs, whiteflies, and mealybugs. Pinch off blooms to encourage bushiness.

Common name: Cosmos, Yellow
Scientific name: *Cosmos sulphureus*
Plant hardiness: Zones 3–11.
Foliage and bloom colors: Brighter than common cosmos with daisylike flowers. Dark-green foliage, finely divided.
Soil needs: Very well-drained loamy, sandy soil. Fertility: average to poor. Neutral 7.0 pH.
Light needs: Full sun.
Water requirement: Water lightly and infrequently. Drought tolerant once established.
Spacing of plants: 12 in. (30 cm) apart.
Tips and care: Deadhead to prolong flowering. Generally pest and disease free. Excellent cutting flower. Nice combined with foliage plants or with other bright flowers such as dahlias.

Common name: Dahlia
Scientific name: *Dahlia* × *hybrida*
Plant hardiness: Zones 9–11.
Foliage and bloom colors: Bright blossoms come in practically every color except blue; some of the most common shades are yellow, orange, pink, red, or white. Foliage consists of dark-green leaves on sturdy stalks.
Soil needs: Moist, well-drained soil. Fertility: rich. Neutral 7.0 pH.
Light needs: Full sun.
Water requirement: Water regularly; don't let soil dry out. Not drought tolerant.
Spacing of plants: 12 in. (30 cm) apart.
Tips and care: Nice with other flowers or alone. Good cutting flower. Watch out for spider mites and grasshoppers.

Common name: Daisy, Gerbera
Scientific name: *Gerbera jamesonii*
Plant hardiness: Zones 9–11.
Foliage and bloom colors: Yellow-eyed with cream, yellow, orange, pink, or red petals. Green leaves with gray undersides are narrow and long.
Soil needs: Moist, well-drained, loamy soil. Fertility: moderately rich. Acid 6.5 pH.
Light needs: Full sun with afternoon shade in extremely hot climates.
Water requirement: Water frequently.
Spacing of plants: 12 in. (30 cm) apart.
Tips and care: Excellent cutting flower. Slit the bottom of the stem before placing in water. Deadhead blooms for longer flowering time. Watch out for snails and slugs.

Common name: Dusty Miller
Scientific name: *Senecio cineraria*
Plant hardiness: Zones 3–10.
Foliage and bloom colors: Silvery gray or white leaves. Flowers are small and insignificant.
Soil needs: Moist, loose, loamy, well-drained soil. Fertility: rich. Feed with liquid fertilizer occasionally. Neutral 7.0 pH.
Light needs: Full to partial sun.
Water requirement: Water frequently; keep soil evenly moist. Do not overwater; overly wet soil can lead to fungal infections. Tolerates some dry spells.
Spacing of plants: 8–10 in. (20–25 cm) apart, but can crowd in a pot.
Tips and care: Silvery foliage sets off bright-colored flowers, especially in a massed grouping. Pinch back for extra bushiness.

Common name: Fuchsia
Scientific name: *Fuchsia* x *hybrida*
Plant hardiness: Zones 6–10.
Foliage and bloom colors: Dangling tubelike flowers in shades of white, pink, red, or purple. Leaves are green and oval.
Soil needs: Moist, well-drained soil. Fertility: rich. Fertilize every two weeks during the growing season. Acid to neutral 6.5–7.0 pH.
Light needs: Partial sun to shade.
Water requirement: Keep soil moist when plant is flowering.
Spacing of plants: Spread is 6 in.–3 ft. (15–90 cm), so space according to type.
Tips and care: No fragrance, but will attract hummingbirds with its funnel shape. Well suited to hanging baskets. Hose down foliage to discourage pests.

Common name: Geranium, Common
Scientific name: *Pelargonium* x *hortorum*
Plant hardiness: Zones 4–10.
Foliage and bloom colors: Big clusters of red, pink, salmon, or white flowers. Leaves are round or heart-shaped, many with an area of darker color.
Soil needs: Moist, well-drained soil. Fertility: moderately rich to rich. Add lime and feed regularly. Neutral 7.0 pH.
Light needs: Full sun.
Water requirement: Water regularly; allow soil to dry out somewhat between waterings.
Spacing of plants: 12–18 in. (30–45 cm) apart.
Tips and care: Pinch back tips to keep plant from becoming scraggly. A readily flowering plant for pots, windowboxes, and planters.

Common name: Geranium, Ivy
Scientific name: *Pelargonium peltatum*
Plant hardiness: Zones 9–10.
Foliage and bloom colors: Clusters of pink, red, lavender, or white flowers with dark markings. Ivy-shaped leaves are bright green.
Soil needs: Moist, light, well-drained soil. Fertility: moderately rich to rich. Enhance with organic matter. Neutral 7.0 pH.
Light needs: Full sun.
Water requirement: Water regularly; allow soil to dry out somewhat between waterings.
Spacing of plants: 12–18 in. (30–45 cm) apart.

Tips and care: Vigorous plants for a windowbox, container, hanging pot, or planter. Pinch back tips once or twice in the spring to encourage branching. Tolerant of ocean breezes. Watch out for aphids.

Common name: Heliotrope
Scientific name: *Heliotropium arborescens*
Plant hardiness: Zone 10.
Foliage and bloom colors: Tiny clusters of flowers ranging from lavender to purple top bushy growth of wrinkled, dark-green, purple-tinged leaves.
Soil needs: Moist, well-drained, loamy soil. Fertility: average. Supplement with peat moss. Neutral 7.0 pH.
Light needs: Full sun.
Water requirement: Water regularly.
Spacing of plants: 12–18 in. (30–45 cm) apart.
Tips and care: A favorite of the Victorians, perfect for an old-fashioned container cottage garden. Watch out for spider mites and whiteflies. Fragrant flowers for pots positioned near the house.

Common name: Impatiens
Scientific name: *Impatiens wallerana*
Plant hardiness: Zones 3–10.
Foliage and bloom colors: Profusely blooming flowers in pink, magenta, mauve, white, salmon, orange, red, or bicolored. Leaves are a glossy deep green with succulent stems.
Soil needs: Moist, well-drained, sandy soil. Fertility: rich. Fertilize lightly every month with an all-purpose fertilizer. Neutral 7.0 pH.
Light needs: Partial sun.
Water requirement: Water regularly.
Spacing of plants: 10–12 in. (25–30 cm) apart.
Tips and care: Perfect for windowboxes, hanging baskets, and containers in shady spots by entryways or under eaves. Pinch during growth to promote bushiness. Combines well with begonias, ferns, hostas, and lilies.

Common name: Lobelia, Edging
Scientific name: *Lobelia erinus*
Foliage and bloom colors: Tiny flowers in shades of light to dark blue, white, or maroon. Simple green leaves.
Plant hardiness: Zones 3–9.
Soil needs: Moist, sandy, well-drained soil Fertility: rich. Supplement with humus; feed monthly. Neutral 7.0 pH.
Light needs: Full sun or partial shade.
Water requirement: Water frequently, especially when hot.
Spacing of plants: 6–9 in. (15–23 cm) apart.
Tips and care: Pinch off tops when seedlings are 1 in. (25 mm) high to encourage growth. In the United States, the blue of this plant is traditionally combined with the red of geranium and white of petunia for a patriotic planting.

Common name: Marigold, Pot
Scientific name: *Calendula officinalis*
Plant hardiness: Zones 2–10.
Foliage and bloom colors: Flowers range from pale cream to yellow, gold, or bright orange. Leaves are broad and a medium green.
Soil needs: Moist, well-drained soil. Fertility: moderately rich. Fertilize and cut back in midsummer to encourage an autumn bloom. Neutral 7.0 pH.
Light needs: Full to partial sun.
Water requirement: Water well during dry spells.
Spacing of plants: 12 in. (30 cm) apart.
Tips and care: Deadhead to prolong bloom. Petals have a spicy smell and can be used as a substitute for saffron. Fairly pest free.

Common name: Monkey Flower
Scientific name: *Mimulus* x *hybridus*
Plant hardiness: Zones 3–10.
Foliage and bloom colors: Flowers are velvety textured and come in red, yellow, or orange. Leaves are serrated and light to medium green in color.
Soil needs: Moist, well-drained soil with humus. Fertility: moderately rich. Enrich with organic matter. Neutral 7.0 pH.
Light needs: Partial to full shade.
Water requirement: Water regularly; keep soil moist.
Spacing of plants: 6 in. (15 cm) apart.
Tips and care: Remove faded blooms to promote further flowering. Spreads quickly to fill hanging baskets and containers. Prefers cool, moist climate.

Common name: Moss Rose
Scientific name: *Portulaca grandiflora*
Plant hardiness: Zones 9–11.
Foliage and bloom colors: Flowers are waxy and round in yellow, orange, red, pink, or white. Leaves are tubular, plump, and medium green.
Soil needs: Dry, sandy, well-drained soil. Fertility: average to poor. Do not fertilize.
Light needs: Water well to establish, then sparingly through-out the season.
Spacing of plants: 6–8 in. (15–20 cm) apart.
Tips and care: A great choice for hot and dry sites such as

sunny patios, terra-cotta pots on a ledge, or as a companion planting to cactus, yucca, and other succulents. Varieties include both upright and trailing growth habits. Inspect frequently for aphids.

Common name: Nasturtium
Scientific name: *Tropaeolum majus*
Plant hardiness: Zones 3–10.
Foliage and bloom colors: Flowers are white, yellow, orange, red, pink, or mahogany. Parasol-shaped leaves are bright green and sometimes streaked with white.
Soil needs: Light, sandy, well-drained soil. Fertility: moderately rich to poor. Tolerates poor soils. Neutral 7.0 pH.
Light needs: Full or partial sun.
Water requirement: Keep soil moist, especially in warm weather. Water every 7–10 days.
Spacing of plants: 8–12 in. (20–30 cm) apart.
Tips and care: Flowers are fragrant and edible, with a peppery taste. Cut back to prolong flowering. Excellent for hanging baskets and windowboxes or, mixed with shrubbery, for containers.

Common name: Nemesia
Scientific name: *Nemesia strumosa*
Plant hardiness: Zones 3–10.
Foliage and bloom colors: Cup-shaped flowers come in white, yellow, red, pink, lavender, blue, or bicolored. Leaves are green and shaped like a lance.
Soil needs: Moist, well-drained soil. Fertility: moderately rich to rich. Feed liberally. Acid to neutral 6.5–7.0 pH.
Light needs: Full sun.
Water requirement: Water regularly, especially during particularly dry spells.
Spacing of plants: 6 in. (15 cm) apart.
Tips and care: Pinch tips of seedlings to encourage bushiness. Nice cutting flower.

Common name: Pansy
Scientific name: *Viola* x *wittrockiana*
Plant hardiness: Zones 3–9.
Foliage and bloom colors: Velvety, flat flowers in purple, maroon, blue, red, yellow, orange, white, or tricolored. Shiny, heart-shaped green leaves.
Soil needs: Moist, loamy, well-drained soil. Fertility: moderately rich. Apply liquid plant food every two weeks. Neutral 7.0 pH.
Light needs: Full sun or afternoon shade.
Water requirement: Water regularly; soil can be soaked.
Spacing of plants: 4–6 in. (10–15 cm) apart.
Tips and care: Great in either sunny or partially shady locations. Works nicely with spring bulbs such as hyacinths or daffodils. Deadhead flowers to keep the bloom going. Makes a charming cut flower for a small bouquet.

Common name: Periwinkle, Madagascar
Scientific name: *Catharanthus roseus*
Plant hardiness: Zones 9–11.
Foliage and bloom colors: Cheerful flowers of white, pink, or rose with a contrasting eye. Glossy green foliage.
Soil needs: Moist, well-drained, sandy or loamy soil. Fertility: rich. Neutral 7.0 pH.
Light needs: Full to partial sun.
Water requirement: Water regularly; do not overwater or plant may rot.
Spacing of plants: 9–12 in. (23–30 cm) apart.
Tips and care: Spreads about 1 ft. (30 cm) in a container or windowbox. Does not require deadheading. Pest free.

Common name: Petunia, Common Garden
Scientific name: *Petunia* x *hybrida*
Plant hardiness: Zones 3–10.
Foliage and bloom colors: Charming round flowers in red, pink, rose, purple, violet-blue, pale yellow, white, or striped combinations. Leaves are small, oval, fuzzy, and green.
Soil needs: Well-drained, loamy soil; tolerates a range of soils. Fertility: moderately rich. Supplement with organic matter. Overfertilization will lead to an abundance of foliage at the expense of flowers. Neutral 7.0 pH.
Light needs: Full or partial sun.
Water requirement: Water regularly when plant is becoming established; allow soil to dry out between waterings.
Spacing of plants: 7–10 in. (18–25 cm) apart.
Tips and care: Deadhead to prolong bloom. Generally pest and disease free. Works well in pots, windowboxes, and hanging baskets.

Common name: Phlox or Texas Pride
Scientific name: *Phlox drummondii*
Plant hardiness: Zones 3–9.
Foliage and bloom colors: Colorful and mildly fragrant blooms of red, pink, salmon, purple, white, or bicolored. Stems are erect and foliage is leafy.
Soil needs: Moist to dry, well-drained soil. Fertility: moderately rich. Feed monthly. Acid to neutral 6.5–7.0 pH.
Light needs: Full sun.
Water requirement: Water regularly during spells of dry weather; keep soil evenly moist.
Spacing of plants: 10–12 in. (25–30 cm) apart. Requires good air circulation to avoid problems with powdery mildew.
Tips and care: Dwarf varieties are excellent for pots and hanging baskets. Shear back to promote new growth. Nice cutting flower.

Common name: Rose-of-China
Scientific name: *Hibiscus rosa-sinensis*
Plant hardiness: Zone 10.
Foliage and bloom colors: Papery scarlet, white, cream, yellow, salmon, or orange flowers. Leaves are olive green and narrow.
Soil needs: Moist, well-drained, loamy soil. Fertility: rich. Feed twice a month to maintain good flower production. Neutral 7.0 pH.
Light needs: Full to partial sun.
Water requirement: Water regularly and heavily while plants are growing and blooming.
Spacing of plants: Spreads 3–4 ft. (90–120 cm), so space accordingly.
Tips and care: Pinch tips to encourage branching. Lives more than 25 years, so cut old wood each spring to limit size and encourage new wood. Prune to keep height under 3 ft. (90 cm). Watch out for aphids.

Common name: Sage, Mealy Blue
Scientific name: *Salvia farinacea*
Plant hardiness: Zones 4–8.
Foliage and bloom colors: Lavender flowers bloom atop tall spikes surrounded by foliage that is silver-gray.
Soil needs: Moist, well-drained, loamy soil. Fertility: average to moderately rich. Feed monthly. Neutral 7.0 pH.
Light needs: Full or partial sun.
Water requirement: Water regularly to keep the plant lush.
Spacing of plants: 12 in. (30 cm) apart.
Tips and care: Flowers provide a nice contrast in a container when paired with lower-growing plants such as geraniums or dusty miller. Attracts bees, butterflies, and hummingbirds.

Common name: Snapdragon, Common
Scientific name: *Antirrhinum majus*
Plant hardiness: Zones 3–11.
Foliage and bloom colors: Two-lipped flowers in bright yellow, orange, pink, magenta, red, white, and more. Leaves are medium green.
Soil needs: Moist, well-drained, loamy soil. Fertility: rich. Neutral 7.0 pH.
Light needs: Full or partial sun.
Water requirement: Water moderately; avoid overhead watering, which will promote rust.
Spacing of plants: 4–6 in. (10–15 cm) apart.
Tips and care: Grows year-round in mild climates. Tolerates frost. Pinch stem tips off when plant reaches 2–4 in. (5–10 cm) tall to promote abundant flowering and a shorter plant. Makes a nice cutting flower. Attracts butterflies.

Common name: Verbena, Garden
Scientific name: *Viola* x *hybrida*
Plant hardiness: Zones 3–10.
Foliage and bloom colors: Star-shaped, densely clustered flowers in bright red, pink, purple, blue, or white blooming off a mat of low-spreading stems.
Soil needs: Moist to dry, well-drained, loamy soil. Fertility: rich to moderately rich. Neutral 7.0 pH.
Light needs: Full sun with some shade in the afternoon in very hot climates.
Water requirement: Water regularly during hot, humid spells to encourage flowering; do not overwater. Keep foliage from getting wet to discourage mildew.
Spacing of plants: 6–12 in. (15–30 cm) apart but can crowd in a pot.
Tips and care: Excellent mixed in a large container or hanging basket with petunias, salvias, and catharanthus. Does well in hot, sunny locations. Remove faded blossoms to encourage new flowers. Generally free of pests and disease, but watch out for spider mites in the heat.

Common name: Violet, Bush
Scientific name: *Browallia speciosa*
Plant hardiness: Zones 10–11.
Foliage and bloom colors: Bright-blue, violet, or white petunialike flowers. Small green leaves.
Soil needs: Moist, well-drained soil. Fertility: rich. Overfertilizing will lead to an overabundance of foliage at the expense of flowers. Neutral 7.0 pH.
Light needs: Partial sun.
Water requirement: Water by misting. Do not overwater. Keep soil moist if plant is exposed to hot sun.
Spacing of plants: 12 in. (30 cm) apart.
Tips and care: Pinch out young growth to encourage bushiness. Will spread and drape over container edges.

Common name: Violet, Persian
Scientific name: *Exacum affine*
Plant hardiness: Zones 6–11.
Foliage and bloom colors: Flowers are blue-violet or white. Glossy green leaves grow in little clumps.
Soil needs: Moist, well-drained soil. Fertility: moderately rich. Fertilize every 2–4 weeks. Neutral 7.0 pH.
Light needs: Full sun.
Water requirement: Keep soil slightly moist. Do not overwater or it will weaken stems. Drought tolerant.
Spacing of plants: 6 in. (15 cm) apart.
Tips and care: Lovely grouped in a windowbox. Tolerant of rain but prefers dry, warm weather. Sweetly scented flowers. Watch out for aphids.

Common name: Wishbone Flower
Scientific name: *Torenia fournieri*
Plant hardiness: Zones 4–11.
Foliage and bloom colors: Purple/lavender and pink/red blooms marked with yellow or white on the lower petal. Compact, bushy foliage with heart-shaped green leaves.
Soil needs: Very moist, well-drained soil. Fertility: rich. Add peat moss or organic matter, especially if soil is sandy or high in clay content. Neutral 7.0 pH.
Light needs: Partial shade to full shade in hot climes; in cooler areas, full sun is fine.
Water requirement: Water regularly and well; but don't allow soil to get soggy.
Spacing of plants: 6–8 in. (15–20 cm) apart.
Tips and care: Great for containers and hanging baskets in shady areas. Pinch back to encourage bushiness. Named after the wishbone-shaped stamens.

Common name: Zinnia, Common
Scientific name: *Zinnia elegans*
Plant hardiness: Zones 4–11.
Foliage and bloom colors: Flowers come in bright white, red, pink, orange, yellow, lavender, or white—everything except blue—and rise on stiff stalks above simple green leaves.
Soil needs: Moist, well-drained, loamy soil. Fertility: moderately rich. Fertilize lightly. Neutral to alkaline 7.0–7.5 pH.
Light needs: Full sun.
Water requirement: Water regularly; avoid wetting foliage as powdery mildew can be a problem.
Spacing of plants: 6–12 in. (15–30 cm) apart. Do not crowd—poor air circulation promotes mildew.
Tips and care: Cut back flowers to increase the bloom. Works well in contrast with softer plants such as petunias or geraniums. Nice cutting flower.

PERENNIALS

Common name: Adam's Needle
Scientific name: *Yucca filamentosa*
Plant hardiness: Zones 5–11.
Foliage and bloom colors: Large, showy white flowers. Sword-shaped, very sharp-tipped leaves with fibers that curl along the edges.
Soil needs: Light, dry, sandy, well-drained soil. Fertility: average. Acid to neutral 6.5–7.0 pH.
Light needs: Full to partial sun.
Water requirement: Water moderately.
Spacing of plants: 10 ft. (3 m) apart. Flower height reaches 5–6 ft. (1.5–1.8 m) tall, but there are smaller cultivars; space accordingly.
Tips and care: Tolerates heat, cold, and wind. Works well in containers placed at an entrance, on a formal terrace, or at a beach house. Very low maintenance—remove dead leaves and flowers as needed.

Common name: Ageratum, Hardy; or Mist Flower
Scientific name: *Eupatorium coelestinum*
Plant hardiness: Zones 5–11.
Foliage and bloom colors: Clusters of baby-blue flowers atop lush and bushy light-green foliage.
Soil needs: Moist, well-drained soil. Sandy loam aids in the spread of this plant, which can reach up to 2 ft. (60 cm) tall; to slow the spread, use a heavier soil. Fertility: average. Neutral 7.0 pH.
Light needs: Full sun to partial shade.
Water requirement: Water regularly; do not allow soil to dry out or it may stunt growth or kill the plant.
Spacing of plants: 12 in. (30 cm) apart.
Tips and care: Best grown as a single specimen in a pot because of its invasive tendencies. Tolerates heat well; also can be used in wet climates.

Common name: Artemisia or Powis Castle
Scientific name: *Artemisia* x *'Powis Castle'*
Plant hardiness: Zones 6–9.
Foliage and bloom colors: Large, lacy mounds of silvery green leaves. Flowers are yellow and insignificant.
Soil needs: Very well-drained loamy soil. Fertility: average. Neutral 7.0 pH.
Light needs: Full sun to partial shade.
Water requirement: Water sparingly; does well under dry, hot conditions. Try to keep leaves from getting or remaining wet.
Spacing of plants: 12–15 in. (30–38 cm) apart.
Tips and care: Subdued foliage makes a good backdrop for brighter-colored plants. Leaves are aromatic. Trim back old shoots in spring to encourage new growth. Well suited to hanging baskets or used as a featured plant in a small island planting.

Common name: Astilbe
Scientific name: *Astilbe* x *arendsii*
Plant hardiness: Zones 4–9.
Foliage and bloom colors: Impressive flower sprays in light pink, dark pink, bright red, or white. Delicate, fernlike foliage with a bronze-green cast.
Soil needs: Moist, well-drained soil. Fertility: rich. Supplement with organic matter; fertilize monthly during the growing season. Acid to neutral 6.5–7.0 pH.
Light needs: Partial sun to shade.
Water requirement: Water regularly and well; keep soil moist.
Spacing of plants: 15–18 in. (38–45 cm) apart.
Tips and care: Best suited to regions with cool summers. Relatively pest free. Divide crowded plants in spring to ensure good flower production. Excellent cutting flower that then can be dried for long-lasting floral arrangements.

Common name: Bear's Breech
Scientific name: *Acanthus mollis*
Plant hardiness: Zones 6–10.
Foliage and bloom colors: Tubular lilac, rose, or white flowers bloom atop large flower spikes. Dark-green, glossy, deeply lobed, large, and lush foliage.
Soil needs: Well-drained, loamy soil. Fertility: average. Neutral 7.0 pH.
Light needs: Full sun to shade.
Water requirement: Water moderately; does not like wet conditions.
Spacing of plants: 3 ft. (90 cm) apart.
Tips and care: Foliage was the inspiration for the classic Greek Corinthian column. Flower colors are highlighted if plant is placed in light shade. Works well combined with ferns and hostas. Elegant cutting flower.

Common name: Bellflower, Serbian
Scientific name: *Campanula poscharskyana*
Plant hardiness: Zones 3–10.
Foliage and bloom colors: Bell-shaped purple flowers bloom from long trailing stems. Leaves are heart-shaped and green.
Soil needs: Moist, well-drained, loamy soil. Fertility: average to moderately rich. Fertilize regularly. Neutral 7.0 pH.
Light needs: Full to partial sun.
Water requirement: Water moderately; tolerates dry and moist soils.
Spacing of plants: 10–12 in. (25–30 cm) apart.
Tips and care: Great in a hanging basket because its trailing stems create a pleasing effect. Easy and fast to grow. Does well by the seashore and in Mediterranean climate areas with conditions similar to those of its natural homeland. Deadhead and trim stems to keep plants neat.

Common name: Bergenia, Heartleaf
Scientific name: *Bergenia cordifolia*
Plant hardiness: Zones 3–10.
Foliage and bloom colors: Dense clumps of thick fleshy leaves are green in summer and turn red in autumn. Clusters of small pink flowers bloom in spring.
Soil needs: Moist, loamy soil; tolerates a range of soils. Fertility: average. Neutral 7.0 pH.
Light needs: Partial shade.
Water requirement: Water regularly.
Spacing of plants: 12–15 in. (30–38 cm) apart.
Tips and care: Substantial foliage contrasts nicely with ferns and astilbes. Leaves are subject to attacks by many pests, including slugs, aphids, snails, and chipmunks.

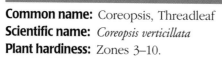

Common name: Calamint
Scientific name: *Calamintha nepeta*
Plant hardiness: Zones 5–10.
Foliage and bloom colors: Pale lavender or white flowers form a pretty cloud over shiny dark grayish-green foliage. Member of the mint family; leaves are very aromatic.
Soil needs: Well-drained, loamy soil. Fertility: average. Neutral 7.0 pH.
Light needs: Full sun to partial shade.
Water requirement: Water moderately.
Spacing of plants: 15–18 in. (38–45 cm) apart.
Tips and care: Fragrance makes this plant a natural for a patio or entryway, but beware: it attracts bees for the same reason. Highly pest and disease resistant. Use it as a midheight groundcover in areas that do not receive foot traffic.

Common name: Coreopsis, Threadleaf
Scientific name: *Coreopsis verticillata*
Plant hardiness: Zones 3–10.
Foliage and bloom colors: Light, golden, daisylike flowers rise above fine threadlike foliage.
Soil needs: Well-drained soil; tolerates a range of soils. Fertility: average. Acid to alkaline 6.5–7.5 pH.
Light needs: Full sun.
Water requirement: Water moderately. Drought tolerant, but watch out for very hot, dry conditions.
Spacing of plants: 12 in. (30 cm) apart.
Tips and care: Remove faded flowers by pinching or trimming off the top of the plant to encourage further blooms. Very nice in a hanging basket. Excellent cutting flower. A hardy, low-maintenance plant.

Common name: Daylily Hybrids
Scientific name: *Hemerocallis*
Plant hardiness: Zones 4–10.
Foliage and bloom colors: Tall flower stalks in cream, yellow, orange, salmon, pink-rose, deep red, purple-red, lavender, or bicolored. Foliage is a dense mound of long and narrow green leaves.
Soil needs: Moist, well-drained, loamy soil. Fertility: moderately rich. Do not overfertilize, which will lead to lusher foliage at the expense of flowers. Neutral 7.0 pH.
Light needs: Full sun.
Water requirements: During the height of summer heat, water at least once a week.
Spacing of plants: Spread is 15–24 in. (38–60 cm), depending on type; space accordingly.
Tips and care: Great for containers in a sunny location. Deadhead to promote new flowers; each flower lasts just a day, but new buds keep blooming for weeks. Very pest and disease resistant. Easy to grow.

Common name: Geranium, Strawberry
Scientific name: *Saxifraga stolonifera*
Plant hardiness: Zones 7–10.
Foliage and bloom colors: Delicate white flower clusters grow out of a mound of leaves that are silver-veined with reddish undersides.
Soil needs: Moist, well-drained, loamy soil. Fertility: moderately rich to rich. Supplement with organic matter such as peat moss, leaf mold, or compost. Neutral to slightly alkaline 7.0–7.5 pH.
Light needs: Light to full shade.
Water requirement: Water regularly.
Spacing of plants: 8–10 in. (20–25 cm) apart.
Tips and care: Spreads quickly, so better potted alone in a hanging basket. Prune runners to hold back growth. Watch out for mealybugs.

Common name: Ice Plant, Purple
Scientific name: *Delosperma cooperi*
Plant hardiness: Zones 6–10.
Foliage and bloom colors: Bright-purple or rose-pink daisylike flowers. Foliage is succulent and grayish-green.
Soil needs: Well-drained soil; tolerates a range of soils. Fertility: average to poor. Neutral to alkaline 7.0–7.5 pH.
Light needs: Full sun.
Water requirement: Water sparingly; does well in dry conditions. Extremely drought tolerant.
Spacing of plants: 10–12 in. (25–30 cm) apart.
Tips and care: Excellent on a sunny patio with other heat-loving succulents or annuals. Will drape over the side of a pot. Low maintenance.

Common name: Japanese Sweet Flag
Scientific name: *Acorus gramineus variegatus*
Plant hardiness: Zones 6–10.
Foliage and bloom colors: Low, fan-shaped, grasslike tufts with narrow white-striped leaves.
Soil needs: Moist, loamy soil. Fertility: average. Do not feed for the first six months, then fertilize twice a year. Slightly acidic to neutral 6.5–7.0 pH.
Light needs: Full sun to partial shade.
Water requirement: Keep soil moist; does very well in a shallow tray of water.
Spacing of plants: 12 in. (30 cm) apart.
Tips and care: Excellent positioned near a pool or fountain. Contrasts nicely with larger-leafed plants. Works well to brighten a shady spot. Leaves are aromatic when crushed. Low maintenance and pest resistant.

Common name: Lavender, English
Scientific name: *Lavandula angustifolia*
Plant hardiness: Zones 4–10.
Foliage and bloom colors: Small lavender flowers bloom off tall spikes. Foliage is gray or blue-green and needlelike. Both flowers and foliage are aromatic.
Soil needs: Dry, well-drained soil. Fertility: average to poor. The poorer the fertility, the more aromatic the plant. Alkaline 7.5 pH.
Light needs: Full sun.
Water requirement: Water regularly; allow the soil to dry out in between waterings.
Spacing of plants: 2–3 ft. (60–90 cm) apart, but can crowd in a pot.
Tips and care: The scent of English lavender is used in sachets, soaps, and perfumes. Stays evergreen in mild climates. Works well in sunny, dry locations.

Common name: Lemon Balm
Scientific name: *Melissa officinalis*
Plant hardiness: Zones 5–9.
Foliage and bloom colors: Aromatic leaves are oval, bright green, and serrated along the edges. Flowers are insignificant. Member of the mint family.
Soil needs: Dry, well-drained, loamy soil. Fertility: poor. Poor soil keeps the scent strong and limits growth. Acid to alkaline 6.5–7.5 pH.
Light needs: Partial sun.
Water requirement: Water moderately; do not overwater.
Spacing of plants: 18 in. (45 cm) apart.
Tips and care: Better planted alone because of invasive tendencies. Can be pruned into an attractive mound shape. Lemony flavor and aroma of the crushed leaves may be used in iced or hot teas. Pinch when young to encourage branching. Watch out for whiteflies.

Common name: Lenten Rose
Scientific name: *Helleborus orientalis*
Plant hardiness: Zones 5–9.
Foliage and bloom colors: Showy cream or purple-pink blossoms and shiny, dark-green, leathery leaves.
Soil needs: Well-drained, moist soil. Fertility: rich. Enrich soil with peat moss, leaf mold, or compost. Neutral to alkaline 7.0–7.5 pH.
Light needs: Partial sun to shade.
Water requirement: Water regularly.
Spacing of plants: 12–15 in. (30–38 cm) apart.
Tips and care: Remove old leaves in spring before flowers appear. Float the large, cup-shaped flowers in water, or cut entire stems for floral bouquets. Pest free.

Warning

Roots of Lenten Rose contain substances that are poisonous if eaten. Exercise care to prevent hazard to children and pets.

Common name: Lilyturf
Scientific name: *Liriope muscari*
Plant hardiness: Zones 5–10.
Foliage and bloom colors: Small lavender or white flowers followed by blue-black berries. Slender, arching dark-green or silver leaves grow in grasslike clumps.
Soil needs: Well-drained, moist, or dry loamy soil mixed with sand. Fertility: average to rich. Acid to neutral 6.5–7.0 pH.
Light needs: Partial sun to full shade; flowers do best with some sun.
Water requirement: Water constantly when establishing; at maturity tolerates dry spells.
Spacing of plants: Spreads to 2 ft. (60 cm), so space accordingly.
Tips and care: Stays evergreen in warm climates. Makes a unique ground cover for planters, where it contrasts nicely with upright plants like yucca. Watch out for slugs and snails.

Common name: Mint, Apple
Scientific name: *Mentha suaveolens*
Plant hardiness: Zones 5–9.
Foliage and bloom colors: This ornamental planting of the mint family has a subtle pineapple scent. Leaves are bright green and white and have a fuzzy texture. Flowers are insignificant.
Soil needs: Moist, loamy soil. Fertility: moderately rich. Feed twice a month. Neutral 7.0 pH.
Light needs: Full sun to shade.
Water requirement: Water regularly; keep soil evenly moist. Will recover if soil dries out.
Spacing of plants: 3 ft. (90 cm) apart.
Tips and care: Not as invasive as other members of the mint family. Beautiful planted with flowering herbs such as white-flowered garlic. Leaves make an edible garnish for salads and drinks. Shear the foliage during the season to renew it.

Common name: Moneywort or Creeping Jenny
Scientific name: *Lysimachia nummularia*
Plant hardiness: Zones 3–9.
Foliage and bloom colors: Bright-green and shiny quarter-sized leaves trail from stems. Bright-yellow flowers about the same size as the leaves sit atop the foliage.
Soil needs: Moist, loamy, well-drained soil. Fertility: moderately rich. Neutral 7.0 pH.
Light needs: Partial to full shade.
Water requirement: Water regularly and well.
Spacing of plants: 12–18 in. (30–45 cm) apart, but can be crowded in a pot.
Tips and care: Good plant for a hanging basket. Makes a pretty carpet in a container with bright flowers such as impatiens and begonias. Pest free.

Common name: Pink, Cottage
Scientific name: *Dianthus* x *allwoodii*
Plant hardiness: Zones 3–9.
Foliage and bloom colors: Flowers with a spicy fragrance in crimson, rose, pink, or white. Leaves are slender and blue-gray and form a mat of foliage.
Soil needs: Well-drained humus. Fertility: rich. Neutral to slightly alkaline 7.0–7.5 pH.
Light needs: Full sun.
Water requirement: Water lightly to moderately; stems and root tops should be kept fairly free of moisture to prevent mildew.
Spacing of plants: 12–18 in. (30–45 cm) apart.
Tips and care: Lovely clovelike fragrance. Attractive next to silvery-foliaged plants such as lavenders and artemisias.

Common name: Primrose, Polyanthus
Scientific name: *Primula* x *polyantha*
Plant hardiness: Zones 3–8.
Foliage and bloom colors: Flowers come in colors from crisp, pure white to pink, red, lavender, purple, and more. Blooms in yellow and orange have a scent. Leaves are light green and have wrinkled edges.
Soil needs: Moist, well-drained soil. Fertility: rich. Supplement with organic matter and feed lightly twice a month. Slightly acid to neutral 6.5–7.0 pH.
Light needs: Partial sun to shade.
Water requirement: Keep soil slightly moist; tolerates dry spells.
Spacing of plants: 12 in. (30 cm) apart.
Tips and care: Easy flowers to grow. Provides very bright color for a gathering of pots. Cut off faded blossoms. Watch out for snails, slugs, and spider mites.

Common name: Ribbon Grass
Scientific name: *Phalaris arundinacea*
Plant hardiness: Zones 4–9.
Foliage and bloom colors: Hard, smooth leaves are bright green and striped with white, turning brown in late summer. Flowers are pinkish white and not notable.
Soil needs: Moist, well-drained loamy soil. Fertility: average. Slightly alkaline 7.5 pH.
Light needs: Full sun to shade.
Water requirement: Needs constant moisture; add peat moss to help retain water.
Spacing of plants: 12 in. (30 cm) apart.
Tips and care: Can be invasive but provides a nice bright spot of color in a dark area or as part of a palette placed near bright flowers. A trouble-free container planting.

Warning

Foliage of Ribbon Grass contains substances that are harmful to humans and pets if ingested Avoid hazard to children and pets.

Common name: Sage, Autumn
Scientific name: *Salvia greggii*
Plant hardiness: Zones 8–10.
Foliage and bloom colors: Scented rose-pink, red, salmon, purple, or white flowers enhance this low bushy plant with small fragrant, semi-evergreen leaves.
Soil needs: Very well-drained sandy or loamy soil. Fertility: moderately rich. Neutral 7.0 pH.
Light needs: Full sun to partial shade.
Water requirement: Water regularly—a bit more during dry spells to encourage flowers.
Spacing of plants: 1–2 ft. (30–60 cm) apart.
Tips and care: Does very well in heat. Attracts butterflies and hummingbirds. Works nicely with blue fescue, oregano, and other Mediterranean-style plants.

BULBS

Common name: Begonia, Tuberous
Scientific name: *Begonia* × *tuberhybrida*
Plant hardiness: Zones 3–10.
Foliage and bloom colors: Large flowers of orange, yellow, red, or pink, sometimes with a contrasting petal edge. Foliage grows to a mound and has a green or bronze color.
Soil needs: Moist, well-drained loamy soil; add peat moss to help retain moisture. Fertility: rich. Fertilize well at least once a month. Slightly acid to neutral 6.5–7.0 pH.
Light needs: Partial sun to shade.
Water requirement: Water regularly; keep soil moist but do not allow it to become soggy.
Spacing of plants: 12–15 in. (30–38 cm) apart.
Tips and care: Available in both cascading and upright forms. Cascading form is lovely in a hanging basket. In cold-winter climates, dig up and replant tubers each year.

Common name: Calla Lily
Scientific name: *Zantedeschia albomaculata*
Plant hardiness: Zones 8–10.
Foliage and bloom colors: Graceful flowers in creamy white, yellow, pink, red, or orange emerge from rolled, white-spotted, dark-green leaves. Stalks are long, and leaves are lance- or arrow-shaped.
Soil needs: Moist, loamy soil. Fertility: rich. Feed every two weeks during the growing season. Neutral 7.0 pH.
Light needs: Partial sun.
Water requirement: Keep soil wet at all times; may be placed in a tray of shallow water or even in a pond.
Spacing of plants: 1–2 ft. (30–60 cm) apart.
Tips and care: A long-lived cutting flower popular in bridal arrangements. Easy to grow. Watch out for spider mites.

Common name: Crocus, Dutch
Scientific name: *Crocus vernus*
Plant hardiness: Zones 5–9.
Foliage and bloom colors: White or lilac flowers with purple stripes in late winter and early spring. Foliage is grasslike and dark green.
Soil needs: Moist, well-drained, loamy soil. Fertility: average to moderately rich. Fertilize when shoots appear, then again after flowers appear. Neutral 7.0 pH.
Light needs: Full to partial sun.
Water requirement: Water moderately; keep soil moist during the blooming periods.
Spacing of plants: 6 in. (15 cm) apart.
Tips and care: Pretty in a mass planting in a low container. Transfer container-grown bulbs to open garden in the second year.

Common name: Cyclamen, Florist's
Scientific name: *Cyclamen persicum*
Plant hardiness: Zones 5–9.
Foliage and bloom colors: Delicate long-stemmed flowers in pink, red, white, or lavender. Leaves are heart-shaped, thick, and dark green with silver markings.
Soil needs: Moist, well-drained soil; mix in loam and sand to help retain moisture. Fertility: rich. Supplement with compost and feed regularly to ensure a robust bloom. Neutral 7.0 pH.
Light needs: Partial sun to shade.
Water requirement: Keep soil evenly moist.
Spacing of plants: 12–18 in. (30–45 cm) apart.
Tips and care: Does best in a pot by itself grouped with flowers such as primroses or ranunculus. Excellent indoor plant. Remove faded flowers and leaves. Watch out for spider mites.

Common name: Daffodil
Scientific name: *Narcissus*
Plant hardiness: Zones 3–9.
Foliage and bloom colors: This very popular bulb comes in white, cream, yellow, orange, or pink.
Soil needs: Moist, loamy, well-drained soil; lace with a coarse sand to improve drainage. Fertility: poor. Neutral 7.0 pH.
Light needs: Full sun to partial shade.
Water requirement: Keep soil moist but not soggy.
Spacing of plants: Large varieties, 6–8 in. (15–20 cm) apart; small varieties, 3–4 in. (8–10 cm) apart.
Tips and care: Low-maintenance, trouble-free plant. Excellent cutting flower. Works well with stock, pansies, and ranunculus. Plant as a border around vegetables to reduce mole and gopher damage.

Warning

Bulbs, leaves, and flowers of Daffodil contain arsenic and are fatal if eaten. Exercise care to prevent hazard to children and pets.

Common name: Iris, Reticulated
Scientific name: *Iris reticulata*
Plant hardiness: Zones 3–8.
Foliage and bloom colors: Early-spring blooms are blue, purple, or lavender, often with orange or yellow markings. Short-stalked with smooth green leaves.
Soil needs: Well-drained, loamy soil. Fertility: average to moderately rich. Neutral 7.0 pH.
Light needs: Full sun.
Water requirement: Water regularly when growth is new, then taper off as plant goes dormant during summer.
Spacing of plants: 2–3 in. (5–8 cm) apart.
Tips and care: Flowers have a grapelike aroma. Remove leaves if they turn yellow. Excellent for small containers.

Common name: Kaffir Lily
Scientific name: *Clivia miniata*
Plant hardiness: Zones 9–11.
Foliage and bloom colors: Funnel-shaped flowers come in deep red-orange and sometimes yellow. Foliage is broad, waxy, and dark green.
Soil needs: Moist, loamy, well-drained soil. Fertility: rich. Enrich soil with organic matter and feed with liquid fertilizer through the growing period. Neutral 7.0 pH.
Light needs: Partial sun to shade.
Water requirement: Water regularly and keep soil moist. Tolerates dry spells.
Spacing of plants: 6–12 in. (15–30 cm) apart.
Tips and care: Early-flowering plant native to South America. Works very well indoors, away from direct sunlight. Containers or baskets under trees or overhangs are good spots for this shade-tolerant flower.

Common name: Lily, Oriental Hybrids
Scientific name: *Lilium*
Plant hardiness: Zones 5–8.
Foliage and bloom colors: Very large flowers of pink, white, red, or gold that are often spotted. Dark-green leaves are tapered and long.
Soil needs: Moist, well-drained soil. Fertility: rich. Acid to neutral 6.5–7.0 pH.
Light needs: Full to partial sun.
Water requirement: Water regularly; don't allow soil to dry out completely.
Spacing of plants: 2 ft. (60 cm) apart.
Tips and care: Large pots with good drainage are the best choice for containers. Watch out for aphids, which spread a virus that can seriously weaken these lilies. Destroy any plants that have disfigured buds or yellow streaks on the leaves.

Common name: Lily-of-the-Nile
Scientific name: *Agapanthus orientalis*
Plant hardiness: Zones 8–11.
Foliage and bloom colors: Stalks bear as many as 100 flowers in blue or white. Leaves are very long, straplike, and evergreen.
Soil needs: Moist, well-drained soil. Fertility: rich. Feed every two weeks during growing period. Neutral 7.0 pH.
Light needs: Full to partial sun.
Water requirement: Keep soil moist. Tolerates drought.
Spacing of plants: 12–24 in. (30–60 cm).
Tips and care: A dramatic accent for containers on terraces and by pools. Excellent, long-lasting cutting flower. After several years, dense colonies of plants will form; divide them by cutting deeply into the cluster with a sharp spade. Watch out for mealybugs.

Common name: Ranunculus, Persian
Scientific name: *Ranunculus asiaticus*
Plant hardiness: Zones 8–10.
Foliage and bloom colors: Brilliantly colored camellialike blooms come in yellow, orange, pink, cream, white, or red—everything except green and blue. Foliage is dark green and fernlike.
Soil needs: Moist, well-drained, loamy soil; add coarse sand to aid drainage. Fertility: poor to average. Neutral 7.0 pH.
Light needs: Full sun.
Water requirement: Keep soil moist.
Spacing of plants: 4–6 in. (10–15 cm) apart.
Tips and care: Great cutting flower. Soak tubers 3–4 hours before planting. Young shoots emerging from containers or pots are a favorite snack for snails and birds, so keep an eye out.

Common name: Tulip
Scientific name: *Tulipa*
Plant hardiness: Zones 4–9.
Foliage and bloom colors: Flowers come in white or a variety of brilliant, intense colors, including red, orange, yellow, pink, purple, bicolored, or multicolored. Stalks are stiff and long; leaves are grayish-green.
Soil needs: Moist, well-drained, loamy soil. Fertility: rich. Fertilize every two weeks during the flowering period.
Light needs: Full sun.
Water requirement: Keep soil moist but not soggy.
Spacing of plants: Until almost touching.
Tips and care: Container-grown bulbs should be planted to open garden in the second year. Beautiful cutting flower. Wash off leaves if aphids are a problem.

FRUITS AND VEGETABLES

Common name: Blueberry, Highbush; and Blueberry, Lowbush
Scientific name: *Vaccinium corymbosum* and *Vaccinium angustifolium*
Plant hardiness: Zones 2–7 (Lowbush hardy to 6).
Foliage and bloom colors: Both varieties have pale-green, bumpy twigs with oval green leaves that turn red in autumn. Flowers are bell-shaped and pink or white. Blue-black fruit appears in spring.
Soil needs: Moist, very well-drained soil, a good deal of which should be peat moss. Fertility: average to poor. Apply a complete acid fertilizer once a year in midspring. Acid 4.5–6.0 pH. Will not grow in alkaline soils.
Light needs: Full sun to partial shade.
Water requirement: Water regularly.
Spacing of plants: Highbush blueberry, 5–6 ft. (1.5–1.8 m) apart; lowbush reaches 12–18 in. (30–45 cm) tall, so space accordingly.
Tips and care: Lowbush blueberry makes a nice ground cover for a container holding tall trees or shrubs. Prune back both types of blueberry in winter or early spring to help fruit production. Buy plants with soil around the roots. Shrubs will produce for 35–40 years. Black plastic netting will keep birds at bay.

Common name: Corn, Sweet
Scientific name: *Zea mays*
Plant hardiness: Zones 4–10.
Foliage and bloom colors: Each silky green cornstalk bears one or two ears of yellow, white, or yellow-and-white corn.
Soil needs: Moist, well-drained soil. Fertility: rich. Enrich soil with manure. Apply liquid fertilizer twice during the growing season. Acid 6.0–6.5 pH.
Light needs: Full sun.
Water requirement: Water regularly or if plant appears to be wilting. Keep soil moist while ears are forming.
Spacing of plants: 6 in. (15 cm) apart.
Tips and care: Corn is ready for picking when the silk at the end of the ear turns brown. Cook and eat corn as soon as possible after picking for the sweetest taste.

Common name: Onion, Common
Scientific name: *Allium cepa*
Plant hardiness: Zones 3–10.
Foliage and bloom colors: Member of the lily family produces mild, sweet, or pungent bulbs that lie close to the surface of the soil. Leaves are blue-green and hollow; the onion skin is white, yellow, or red.
Soil needs: Moist, well-drained soil. Fertility: rich. Supplement with manure and compost and fertilize twice—once when onions are 6 in. (15 cm) tall and again when 12 in. (30 cm) tall. Acid to neutral 5.5–7.0 pH.
Light needs: Full sun.
Water requirement: Water regularly and well; keep roots moist.
Spacing of plants: 2–4 in. (5–10 cm) apart.
Tips and care: The Egyptians first cultivated the onion, and the Spanish brought it to North America. When leaves turn yellow, "lodge," or bend the stems horizontally, to stop growth and allow the bulbs to ripen.

Common name: Peach
Scientific name: *Prunus persica*
Plant hardiness: Zones 5–9.
Foliage and bloom colors: Dark-green lance-shaped leaves and pink to deep-red flowers frame the fuzzy red- and yellow-skinned fruit, which ripens by midsummer.
Soil needs: Moist, well-drained, loamy soil. Fertility: average to moderately rich. Apply a complete fertilizer once a month from spring through summer. Slightly acid to neutral 6.0–7.0 pH.
Light needs: Full sun.
Water requirement: Keep soil moist but not soggy.
Spacing of plants: Standard trees grow 12–15 ft. (3.5–4.5 m) tall; dwarf varieties 3–4 ft. (90–120 cm) or 6–7 ft. (1.8–2 m) tall. Space accordingly.
Tips and care: Pick fruit when it can be separated easily from the twig. Thin out branches by pruning, which will encourage less yield but more flavorful fruit. Store peaches in a cool place, and don't let them touch each other.

Common name: Strawberry
Scientific name: *Fragaria*
Plant hardiness: Zones 3–10.
Foliage and bloom colors: Green serrated leaves and small white flowers yield to fuzzy, seeded, sweet red fruit.
Soil needs: Moist, well-drained soil. Fertility: rich. Supplement with compost and manure. Fertilize every two weeks from spring to autumn. Acid 5.5–6.5 pH.
Light needs: Full sun.
Water requirement: Water regularly; keep soil moist but not soggy. Watered frequently in hot, dry weather.
Spacing of plants: 12–24 in. (30–60 cm) apart.
Tips and care: May also be grown in hanging baskets. A low tent of plastic netting will discourage birds from getting to fruit. Keep fruit off soil surface. Cut off stray runners in autumn to conserve the plant's energy.

Common name: Tomato
Scientific name: *Lycopersicon lycopersicum*
Plant hardiness: Zones 2–11.
Foliage and bloom colors: Hundreds of varieties sport the red, round, classic fruit, which also comes in yellow, orange, or striped varieties. Leaves are green; stems can get somewhat scraggly and may need to be staked to support fruit.
Soil needs: Moist, well-drained soil. Fertility: rich. Supplement with compost or manure and feed once a month. Slightly acid 6.2–6.8 pH is best; neutral to alkaline 7.0–7.5 pH is acceptable.
Light needs: Full sun.
Water requirement: Water regularly.
Spacing of plants: 18–24 in. (45–60 cm) apart in general, but follow guidelines for the particular variety.
Tips and care: Plant tomatoes with carrots, celery, onions, and pot marigold, which will help deter worms. Tomatoes are ready to be harvested when they reach their full, ripe color. Prune plants when they become too heavy to train on a stake.

HERBS

Common name: Basil
Scientific name: *Ocimum basilicum*
Plant hardiness: Zones 3–11.
Foliage and bloom colors: Shiny, silky, highly aromatic and flavorful green leaves. Spirals of white or purple flowers bloom from narrow spikes.
Soil needs: Moist, well-drained, loamy soil. Fertility: moderately rich. Supplement soil with compost or manure. Acid to alkaline 6.5–7.5 pH.
Light needs: Full to partial sun.
Water requirement: Keep soil moist.
Spacing of plants: 8–10 in. (20–25 cm) apart.
Tips and care: Prefers hot weather. Great in pots or windowboxes near the kitchen. Pinch tops to encourage bushiness. Store by freezing or by packing into jars with olive oil, and then refrigerating. Works well with tomatoes, in a pesto sauce, and as a garnish.

Common name: Bay, Sweet
Scientific name: *Laurus nobilis*
Plant hardiness: Zones 8–10.
Foliage and bloom colors: Evergreen leaves are stiff, oval, flat, dark green, and fragrant when crushed.
Soil needs: Moist, well-drained, loamy soil. Fertility: poor to moderately rich. Feed lightly in spring and early summer. Acid to alkaline 6.5–7.5 pH.
Light needs: Full sun.
Water requirement: Water moderately; will recover from dried-out soil. Mist leaves to keep them fresh.
Spacing of plants: 14–16 in. (35–40 cm) apart.
Tips and care: Use whole leaves in stews and soups. Leaves placed in closets help prevent damage from silverfish. Bring containers indoors when temperatures fall below 20°F (-7°C).

Common name: Chives
Scientific name: *Allium schoenoprasum*
Plant hardiness: Zones 3–10.
Foliage and bloom colors: Thin, hollow, grasslike leaves that are bright and dark green. Globe-shaped deep-pink or purple flowers pop above the leaves on thin stalks.
Soil needs: Moist, well-drained, loamy soil. Fertility: average to rich. Acid to neutral 6.0–7.0 pH.
Light needs: Full to partial sun.
Water requirement: Keep soil moist throughout the growing season.
Spacing of plants: 12 in. (30 cm) apart.
Tips and care: Excellent in egg dishes, cheese dishes, salads, soups, and sour-cream mixes. Chives are easy to use and grow—just snip the leaves off with a pair of scissors. Remove flower heads to increase flavor. Flowers make a nice garnish and are edible but have a strawlike texture.

Common name: Mint
Scientific name: *Mentha*
Plant hardiness: Zones 3–10.
Foliage and bloom colors: The most popular varieties are spearmint (*M. spicata*) and peppermint (*M. x piperita*). Both have crinkled, tooth-edged, intensely fragrant leaves. Tiny violet or pink blooms rise on flower spikes.
Soil needs: Moist, well-drained, loamy soil. Fertility: rich. Supplement with compost and fertilize twice a month. Acidic 5.5–6.5 pH.
Light needs: Full sun to partial shade.
Water requirement: Keep soil moist; will recover from dried-out soil.
Spacing of plants: 12–15 in. (30–38 cm) apart.
Tips and care: A very invasive plant more suited to container gardening. Excellent for use in sauces, drinks, desserts, and as a breath freshener. Watch out for caterpillars.

Common name: Oregano
Scientific name: *Origanum vulgare*
Plant hardiness: Zones 3–10.
Foliage and bloom colors: A lush mat of dark-green foliage on woody stems. Flowers are pink or white on spikes.
Soil needs: Moist, well-drained soil. Fertility: moderately rich. Apply a complete fertilizer monthly. Acid to alkaline 6.5–7.5 pH.
Light needs: Full sun; the more sun, the more intense the flavor.
Water requirement: Keep soil moist but not soggy.
Spacing of plants: 8–10 in. (20–25 cm) apart.
Tips and care: Because of its spreading properties, nice in hanging baskets. Leaves can be used either fresh or dried. Add oregano when cooking in the last stages; if cooked too long it can become bitter. Good in sauces, cheese dishes, poultry dishes, pastas, and pizza. Harvest leaves and stem tips after flower buds form and when plant is 4–5 in. (10–13 cm) tall.

Common name: Rosemary
Scientific name: *Rosmarinus officinalis*
Plant hardiness: Zones 8–11.
Foliage and bloom colors: Highly aromatic grayish-green leaves that look like pine needles. Tiny pale-blue flowers.
Soil needs: Dry, well-drained, loamy soil. Fertility: average to moderate. Feed once every three weeks during spring and summer. Neutral to alkaline 7.0–7.5 pH.
Light needs: Full sun.
Water requirement: Keep soil very slightly moist; do not overwater, and do not allow soil to dry out.
Spacing of plants: 6–12 in. (15–35 cm) apart.
Tips and care: Harvest as needed for use in cooking; perfect in lamb, fish, and rice dishes and to include in a bouquet garni. Dried rosemary can be used for sachets or potpourri. Works well for wreaths. Clip thick shrubs to keep growth in check, and pinch back tips to keep plant bushy.

Common name: St. John's Wort
Scientific name: *Hypericum perforatum*
Plant hardiness: Zones 5–9.
Foliage and bloom colors: Clusters of golden-yellow flowers with feathery stamens. Dark-green leaves form a dense mound of foliage and have oil glands that look like small perforations.
Soil needs: Dry or sandy, well-drained soil. Fertility: average. Alkaline 7.5 pH.
Light needs: Full sun to partial shade.
Water requirement: Water sparingly to moderately.
Spacing of plants: Plant reaches 12–36 in. (30–90 cm) tall, so space accordingly.
Tips and care: The most popular prescription drug in Germany for the treatment of mild depression. Also used medicinally to heal wounds. Cut flowers when they open and pick leaves as needed for brewing tea.

DECIDUOUS SHRUBS

Common name: Azaleas, Deciduous
Scientific name: *Rhododendron*
Plant hardiness: Zones 5–11.
Foliage and bloom colors: Fragrant flowers in red, yellow, white, pink, purple, or orange. Small leaves turn bright and colorful in autumn.
Soil needs: Moist, well-drained, humus. Fertility: moderately rich. Supplement with peat moss or leaf mold. Acid 4.5–5.5 pH.
Light needs: Partial sun to partial shade; too much shade will lead to decreased flower production.
Water requirement: Keep soil moist but not soggy.
Spacing of plants: 16–24 in. (40–60 cm) apart.
Tips and care: Excellent container plants for areas where soil or climate conditions preclude in-ground plantings. Hardy, low maintenance, and disease resistant. Remove faded flowers to prevent seed production.

Common name: Crape Myrtle
Scientific name: *Lagerstroemia indica*
Plant hardiness: Zones 7–10.
Foliage and bloom colors: Small flowers with a crinkled, crepe-paper-textured bloom in large clusters of pink, lavender, rosy-red, or white. Small leaves unfurl to a bronze color, turning deep green, then red or orange in autumn.
Soil needs: Moist, well-drained soil. Fertility: moderately rich. Supplement with peat moss or leaf mold. Neutral 7.0 pH.
Light needs: Full to partial sun.
Water requirement: Keep soil moist; will recover from dried-out soil.
Spacing of plants: 4–5 ft. (1.2–1.5 m) apart.
Tips and care: Very attractive lining a driveway or entrance. Does very well in hot weather. Prune in spring to shape and encourage flowers.

Common name: Hydrangea, French
Scientific name: *Hydrangea macrophylla*
Plant hardiness: Zones 6–10.
Foliage and bloom colors: Handsome, round flower heads of pink, blue, purple, or red. Color is determined by the soil's pH. Leaves are broad, oval, and dark green.
Soil needs: Moist, well-drained, loamy soil. Fertility: rich. Supplement with compost, peat moss, or leaf mold. Acid to alkaline 6.5–7.5 pH. Blue and purple flowers bloom in acidic soil—use aluminum sulfate to acidify. Reds and pinks are encouraged by neutral to alkaline conditions—fortify soil with lime.
Light needs: Full to partial sun.
Water requirement: Keep soil moist; do not allow soil to dry out between waterings.
Spacing of plants: 6–10 ft. (2–3 m) apart.
Tips and care: A hardy shrub that looks great in a large pot on the patio or by an entryway. Trouble free and long lived. Does well by the seashore. Cut and dry flower heads for wreaths and floral arrangements.

Common name: Rose, Miniature
Scientific name: *Rosa*
Plant hardiness: Zones 3–10.
Foliage and bloom colors: Penny- to quarter-sized fragrant flowers in shades and blends of pink, red, yellow, and many other colors. Tiny green leaves.
Soil needs: Moist, well-drained, loamy soil. Fertility: moderately rich to rich. Supplement soil with organic matter. Feed every 7–10 days. Acid to neutral 6.5–7.0 pH.
Light needs: Full sun.
Water requirement: Water moderately; do not allow soil to dry out between waterings, and avoid wetting leaves.
Spacing of plants: 12 in. (30 cm) apart.
Tips and care: Charming in hanging baskets or windowboxes. Choose from more than 200 varieties. Prune regularly to shape.

Common name: Rose, Shrub
Scientific name: *Rosa*
Plant hardiness: Zones 3–10.
Foliage and bloom colors: Blooms, some of which are scented, come in rose, pink, white, red, yellow, orange, or purple. Leaves usually are dark green.
Soil needs: Moist, well-drained, loamy soil. Fertility: poor to moderately rich. Feed every 7–10 days with water-soluble fertilizer. Acid to neutral 6.5–7.0 pH.
Light needs: Full sun.
Water requirement: Water moderately; do not allow soil to dry out between waterings, and avoid wetting leaves.
Spacing of plants: 3–5 ft. (90–150 cm) apart.
Tips and care: Prune to shape.

EVERGREEN SHRUBS AND TREES

Common name: Camellia, Common
Scientific name: *Camellia japonica*
Plant hardiness: Zones 8–10.
Foliage and bloom colors: Many-petaled red, white, pink, or multi-colored flowers. Shiny, dark-green oval leaves.
Soil needs: Moist, well-drained soil. Fertility: rich. Supplement with organic matter. Acid 6.5 pH.
Light needs: Partial sun to shade.
Water requirement: Keep soil evenly moist.
Spacing of plants: 2 ft. (60 cm) or more apart, depending on variety.
Tips and care: A handsome container plant for the patio or entryway. Makes a nice screen in front of walls or fencing. Keep sheltered from wind. Avoid fertilizing or pruning once buds have set to avoid premature flower drop.

Common name: Citrus Trees
Scientific name: *Citrus*
Plant hardiness: Zones 9–11.
Foliage and bloom colors: Shiny, bright-green leaves and intensely fragrant blossoms. Flowers are white or pale pink. Fruit is eye-catching.
Soil needs: Moist, well-drained, loamy soil. Fertility: moderately rich. Apply fertilizer once a month. Acid 6.0–6.5 pH.
Light needs: Full sun to partial shade.
Water requirement: Keep soil moist but not soggy.
Spacing of plants: Dwarf citrus grow 4–10 ft. (1.2–3.5 m) tall; non-dwarf varieties, 10–35 ft. (3.5–10.5 m) tall. Space accordingly.
Tips and care: The fruit of dwarf varieties is full sized. Citrus trees can live up to 100 years. Let fruit ripen on the tree; cut it off flush with the button (where the fruit meets the stem). Avoid pruning citrus except when growth becomes leggy.

Common name: Sage, Texas
Scientific name: *Leucophyllum frutescens*
Plant hardiness: Zones 8–9.
Foliage and bloom colors: A mound of grayish foliage made up of fuzzy, silvery leaves. In summer, small bell-shaped, bright pink-purple flowers bloom.
Soil needs: Well-drained, loamy soil mixed with sand. Fertility: poor to average. Neutral 7.0 pH.
Light needs: Full sun.
Water requirement: Water minimally, but good waterings during the bloom season will bring out a lush growth of flowers. Drought tolerant.
Spacing of plants: 4–6 ft. (1.2–1.8 m) apart.
Tips and care: Clay or wood containers are best. Tolerates wind but will not thrive under humid or cool conditions. Subdued foliage makes a good backdrop for colorful flowers. Cut branches back if plant gets scraggly.

VINES

Common name: Jasmine, Star
Scientific name: *Trachelospermum jasminoides*
Plant hardiness: Zones 8–11.
Foliage and bloom colors: Shiny oval leaves and star-shaped, white, intensely fragrant flowers.
Soil needs: Moist, well-drained, loamy soil. Fertility: average. Feed every 2–3 months. Neutral 7.0 pH.
Light needs: Full sun to partial shade.
Water requirement: Water moderately, increasing frequency during dry spells.
Spacing of plants: 8–12 in. (20–30 cm) apart.
Tips and care: Trained up a trellis, will grow up to 15 ft. (4.5 m) high. Also works well in hanging baskets. The perfume can scent an entire garden. Prune out woody stems to renew growth.

Common name: Mandevilla
Scientific name: *Mandevilla* x *amabilis*
Plant hardiness: Zones 10–11.
Foliage and bloom colors: Semitropical vine with large, oval, dark-green leaves and trumpet-shaped pink flowers.
Soil needs: Moist, well-drained, sandy soil. Fertility: rich. Feed every 3–4 weeks with liquid or solid fertilizer. Neutral 7.0 pH.
Light needs: Full sun; afternoon shade is fine.
Water requirement: Keep soil evenly moist during growing season; do not overwater.
Spacing of plants: 2–3 ft. (60–90 cm) apart.
Tips and care: A summer patio plant that can look quite formal or be trained to climb a trellis. Blooms all summer until the first frost. Prune to shape or cut back on growth. Watch out for whiteflies, mealybugs, and spider mites.

Common name: Morning Glory, Common
Scientific name: *Ipomoea purpurea*
Plant hardiness: Zones 9–11.
Foliage and bloom colors: A flowering vine with flowers in blue, pink, lavender, red, or white. Leaves are heart-shaped and medium green.
Soil needs: Moist, well-drained soil; tolerates a range of soils. Fertility: rich. Feed with a low-nitrogen fertilizer to bring out the best flowers and avoid an overabundance of foliage. Neutral 7.0 pH.
Light needs: Full sun.
Water requirement: Water moderately. Tolerates some dryness.
Spacing of plants: Can grow to 15 ft. (4.5 m), so space accordingly.
Tips and care: Perfect for the patio or balcony, where it can be trained to climb and cover a trellis or railing. Also works in hanging baskets. Crowding of roots in containers helps promote flower production.

WATER PLANTS

Common name: Water Lily
Scientific name: *Nymphaea*
Plant hardiness: Zones 4–11.
Foliage and bloom colors: Flowers come in white, yellow, red, purple, or pink. Leaves are round, flat, and green.
Soil needs: Plant in 6-in. (15-cm) plastic pots and fill with garden loam. Position so pot tops are about 6 in. (15 cm) under water. If submerging plants in a wooden container, first fill container with water and add a cup of lime to neutralize the wood's acid; wait a few days before submerging plants.
Light needs: Full sun.
Water requirement: Keep water clean by planting with other oxygenating plants. Water can be 50°F (10°C) for hardy varieties, 70°F (21°C) for tropical.
Spacing of plants: As many pots as your container will hold.
Tips and care: Planter choices for water lily include other water plants are half-barrels, long wooden planters, ceramic fishbowls, and any other watertight container. A goldfish or two added to the water will keep it free of bugs. Running water will interfere with a water lily's bloom.

Common name: Water Parsley
Scientific name: *Oenanthe javanica*
Plant hardiness: Zones 8–11.
Foliage and bloom color: Slender, hollow, erect stems with deep-green leaves that smell like carrot tops and look like celery. Flowers are tiny, white, and fragrant.
Soil needs: Root in moist sand or soil. Fertilize once a week using a water-soluble fertilizer.
Light needs: Sun to shade.
Water requirement: Submerge container so that stems, not foliage, are covered by water.
Spacing of plants: 9 in. (23 cm) apart.
Tips and care: Found wild in freshwater marshes. Can float in containers or on ponds. Tops can be eaten raw and used in salads.

U.S.D.A. Plant Hardiness Zones
of North America

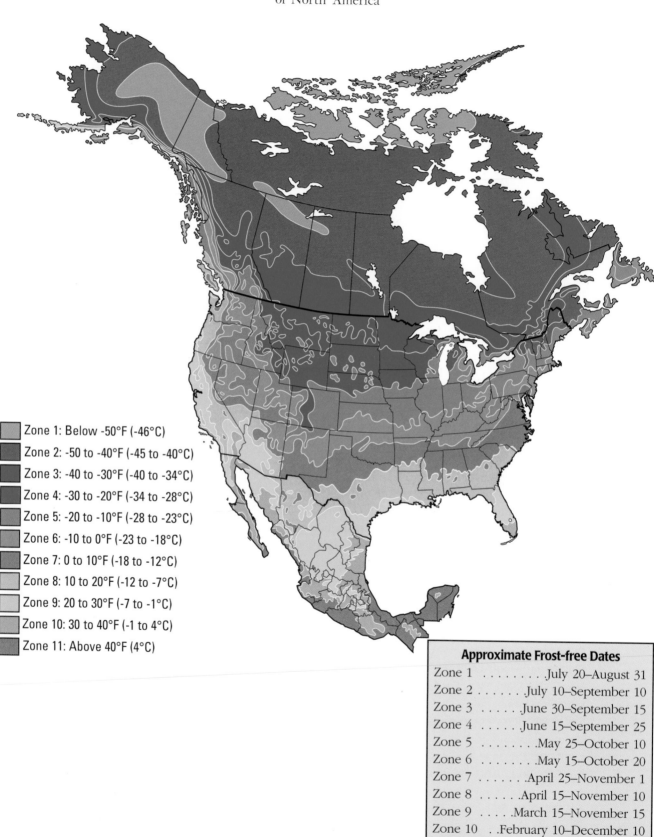

Zone 1: Below -50°F (-46°C)

Zone 2: -50 to -40°F (-45 to -40°C)

Zone 3: -40 to -30°F (-40 to -34°C)

Zone 4: -30 to -20°F (-34 to -28°C)

Zone 5: -20 to -10°F (-28 to -23°C)

Zone 6: -10 to 0°F (-23 to -18°C)

Zone 7: 0 to 10°F (-18 to -12°C)

Zone 8: 10 to 20°F (-12 to -7°C)

Zone 9: 20 to 30°F (-7 to -1°C)

Zone 10: 30 to 40°F (-1 to 4°C)

Zone 11: Above 40°F (4°C)

Approximate Frost-free Dates
Zone 1 . . . . July 20–August 31
Zone 2 . . . . July 10–September 10
Zone 3 . . . . . June 30–September 15
Zone 4 . . . . . June 15–September 25
Zone 5 . . . . .May 25–October 10
Zone 6 . . . . .May 15–October 20
Zone 7 . . . . . .April 25–November 1
Zone 8 . . . . . .April 15–November 10
Zone 9 . . . . .March 15–November 15
Zone 10 . .February 10–December 10
Zone 11 . . . . .Frost-free All Year

The United States Department of Agriculture (USDA) Plant Hardiness Zone Map provides a general guide to growing conditions in North America. It divides the continent into 11 zones based on average minimum annual temperatures within each zone. The zones roughly predict which plants will survive in a given area.

True annual plants are genetically programmed to live for no more than a year, regardless of where they're planted, so hardiness zones mainly affect them by limiting the length of the growing season. Perennials or biennials, on the other hand, grow only in the zones where they've adapted to the climate. In marginal zones, perennials and biennials also will die at the end of the season.

When you're planting a container garden, you don't necessarily need to worry about minimum temperature zones. Plants in containers can be moved into sheltered areas. Your major concern more likely will be the first and last frost dates in your area [see chart, opposite]. Sow seed indoors for cold-season plants—those that tolerate soil temperatures for germination of 40–50° F (4–10° C)—six weeks before the last frost, while waiting a few more weeks for warm-season plants—those that prefer planting temperatures of 60° F (16° C) or higher. The average first and last frost dates for your area are guidelines, however, not guarantees.

Moreover, zone maps and frost charts alike can't account for the effects of thermal belts, nearby bodies of water, and other factors that create microclimates within zones [see Microclimates, pg. 132]. Only careful observation will give you an accurate picture of climatic conditions in your own backyard.

Climate and microclimate govern plant choices when gardens are planned and planted

Appendix

Find your plant hardiness zone on the U.S.D.A. scale by identifying your locale, noting its color, and comparing that color to the legend. Remember that local conditions— shade, slope of site, prevailing winds, or other factors—may cause your garden to vary from the surrounding area by a zone or more.

Climate

Severe cold or heat can doom many plants, and even a short bout of pelting rain or punishing wind can wreak havoc in a garden. To see your plants through such tough times, give them a fighting chance against the normal vicissitudes of weather when they're little and stand ready to protect them from extreme conditions as they grow.

The best way to prevent weather-induced garden failure is to plant at the proper time. Warm-season species planted too early may be killed by cold or may never germinate; cool-season ones planted too late will have limited blooms or fail in summer heat.

Shrubs, trees, and other long-lived plants have adapted their growth to preferred climate conditions. During a sustained period of mild-winter conditions, plants classified to warmer hardiness zones may thrive in a cooler zone; though any return to normal winter temperatures will kill them promptly.

By planting in containers, gardeners can choose naturally sheltered sites for warmth-loving species. True subtropical plants, for which a single bite of frost would prove fatal, may be moved indoors or otherwise protected from cold air temperatures.

Remember that container plantings will warm more quickly than in-ground garden soil in the spring but will cool equally fast when air temperatures drop. Insulate your pots if you expect a bout of variable weather.

Microclimates

Much ado is made regarding microclimates, so what are they? Simply put, they are the local conditions that affect the growth of plants in your garden compared to neighboring yards or nearby gardens.

Every garden is affected by the amount of sunlight it receives, both in the intensity of the rays and in the hours of exposure. Gardens with less sunlight are cooler, less-welcoming places for heat-loving plants. Sloped sites cause sunlight to diffuse across a broader area than is experienced on a flat site. Your facing is also important: south-facing gardens receive more sun than those facing in any other direction. All these things add up to your microclimate—or local growing conditions. The regional and local differences of your site are important determinants of garden success.

Heat Zones

There are other guides to help container gardeners choose plants that are well suited to their area. The American Horticultural Society has performed an analysis of the effects of summer heat on plants in many different locales. The result of this research has been reflected in the society's Heat Zone Map [see opposite], which classifies various areas of the United States by the average number of days per year each are will experience temperatures exceeding 86°F (30°C).

That temperature was chosen because of its significance on the growth of plants: higher temperatures cause breakdown of plant cellular proteins, causing distress. The greater the number of days during which temperatures exceed the mark, the more likely that warm-season plantings will succeed—to a point. If temperatures are too high, of course, many plants cannot survive without protection or shelter from sun and heat.

Consult the map when considering purchase of a plant for your container garden. Like the U.S.D.A. Plant Hardiness Zone Map [see pg. 130], find your area on the map, note its color, and match that color with the legend to determine your heat zone.

Many garden suppliers now heat-rate their plants. Look for information about hardiness zone or heat zone on plant tags, seed packages, in catalog descriptions, or other sources of information about your purchase.

Remember that local conditions are variable, however—in any given year, the number of days of heat may rise or fall as much as 20 percent; maximum low temperatures similarly may vary up or down from year to year.

When in doubt, ask an experienced gardener or in-store expert for advice about your region's conditions. Most garden retailers have knowledgeable sales staff able to consult on plant purchases and provide you with planting and growing tips.

Plant Heat-Zone Map
Compiled by the American Horticultural Society

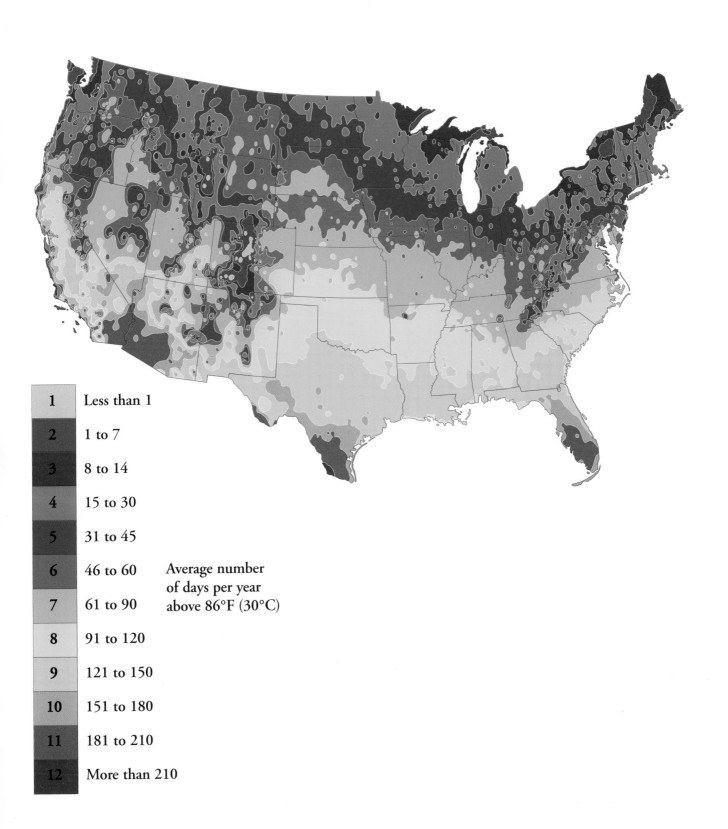

1	Less than 1
2	1 to 7
3	8 to 14
4	15 to 30
5	31 to 45
6	46 to 60
7	61 to 90
8	91 to 120
9	121 to 150
10	151 to 180
11	181 to 210
12	More than 210

Average number
of days per year
above 86°F (30°C)

ON-LINE

INDEX

INDEX

I N D E X